D0931171

QM2

QUEEN
MARY 2
THE BIRTH OF A LEGEND

QUEEN MARY 2

QUEEN MARY 2: THE BIRTH OF A LEGEND

PHOTOGRAPHS BY PHILIP AND GUILLAUME PLISSON WITH ASSISTANCE FROM CHRISTOPHE LE POTIER

Text by Gwen-Haël Denigot and Eric Flounders Captions by Jean-Rémy Villageois, Philip Plisson, and Gwen-Haël Denigot

Translated from the French by Simon Jones

HARRY N. ABRAMS, INC., PUBLISHERS

PREFACE

PREFACE

The story begins in June 1989, when I was on a reporting assignment at Chantiers de l'Atlantique as part of the bicentenary of the French Revolution. The shipyard was within a few weeks of delivering the Brittany Ferries flagship, *Bretagne*. As a gesture of thanks for my interest in the yard, the communications director made me a gift of one of the last of the sumptuous brochures produced exclusively for those invited to the launch of the liner *France* on 11 May 1960. It was published by the master printers Draeger Frères of Montrouge, on 6 May 1960. Ever since, I have lovingly kept this precious document in my bookcase. It is a relic, richly illustrated by the doyen of all French Navy painters, Albert Brenet, who portrayed the shipbuilding industry of Saint-Nazaire.

The construction of the *France* by Albert Brenet

When I heard that the biggest liner of all time was to be built at Saint-Nazaire, I had the idea of following in the footsteps of the master, Albert Brenet, and rediscovering the tradition of the French Navy painters, whose tasks included recording the construction of His Majesty's ships. This personal quest became a reality when Patrick Boissier, president of Alstom Chantiers de l'Atlantique, was also inspired by the idea and gave me his permission to spend twenty-three months living at the heart of the project, under the best possible working conditions. And so, day and night, our mobile home was a part of this industrial landscape, following the great stages of the construction of this colossal puzzle, made up of more than 100 blocks, some weighing more than 600 tonnes.

It had been more than thirty years since a transatlantic liner was built at the shipyard. The last château of the Loire would take shape before our very eyes: the 109th liner and 612th vessel to be built at Saint-Nazaire since 1861.

The *Queen Mary*, a vessel that ruled the oceans, was launched on the river Clyde, in Scotland, in the presence of King George V and Queen Mary. Placed on the stocks in 1930, she made her inaugural crossing in May 1936.

The *France* was laid on the stocks in October 1957, launched on 11 May 1960, and delivered to Le Havre, her home port, in November 1961. The *Queen Mary 2* left her dry dock early on a misty morning in March 2003. She took to the water for the first time in the river Loire, on her way to the fitting-out dock, a mere fourteen months after the first plate was cut and just nine months before she was delivered to Cunard on 22 December 2003.

On board *Pêcheur d'Images IV*, we experienced the first sea trials off Belle-Îsle—a memorable close-up view—and the liner's early-morning returns to land. Most important, however, we accompanied the *Queen Mary 2* on her departure from Saint-Nazaire, with Pamela Conover, president of Cunard; Micky Arison, chairman of the Carnival Corporation, world leader in cruise ships and owner of the *Queen Mary 2*; and Patrick Boissier, president of Alstom Chantiers de l'Atlantique. These three were the architects of this fabulous industrial adventure, which I was fortunate enough to record with the help of my son Guillaume and my faithful assistant, Christophe.

Here we share with you a few images of this work, taken in homage to the women and men who, for twenty-three months, brought this legend to life before our camera lenses.

Photographically yours,
Philip Plisson

A memorable face-to-face meeting on 26 September 2003,
50 nautical miles south of Belle-Îsle

A NEW GOLDEN AGE

THE *QUEEN MARY 2*: A SHIP FOR A NEW GOLDEN AGE

Transatlantic. . .the word itself evokes visions of a boundless ocean, distant lands, and high adventure, perhaps in the mould of a Jules Verne novel. It conjures images of the old steamships, where first-class passengers travelled in palatial luxury alongside emigrants making the crossing to start a new life. We can try to imagine what it must have been like to live in this enclosed universe, suspended between the Old World and the New. If we combine "transatlantic" with "liner," the two together exert the powerful pull of the sea.

On board the RMS *Queen Mary* 2, the most recent addition to this long line of legendary ships, the sea voyage recaptures its mythical stature, symbolised by the vessel's towering, V-shape stem. It is a multidimensional voyage.

This is a voyage back in time, first of all: back to the first half of the last century, to the golden age of the great liners that played such a fabulous role in defining the art of living well. It is also a voyage marked by the passage of time—a long-distance ocean crossing in which the far shore approaches at its own steady pace. Boarding a transatlantic liner is not like embarking on a Caribbean cruise: it means to cross the ocean, to set sail for New York, or the Cape of Good Hope. In an age of instant global communications and universal air travel, it is a rare privilege to regain possession of time and reinvent it.

In true Cunard tradition, passengers on board the *QM2* will see the vastness of the ocean seascape matched by the evocative luxury of the ship's Art Deco interior. To sail past ice floes; to cross paths with schools of dolphins or, with luck, whales; to spy the coast of Africa or Asia through the dawn mist; to enter New York Harbour and admire the Statue of Liberty from the observation deck at the ship's bows (a magical place if ever there was one)—all these are unforgettable moments that perfectly complement the splendour of balls on board, the pleasure of discovering a rare book in the library, the magic of starry nights in the planetarium.

A true giant of the seas, the *QM2* is the longest liner ever built. The ship measures 1132 feet (345 metres)—148 feet (45 metres) longer than the Eiffel Tower is high, and 112 feet (34 metres) longer than the first *Queen Mary*. It is also the widest (135 feet, or 41 metres), tallest (236 feet high, or 72 metres, the equivalent of a twenty-three-storey building), biggest (fifteen decks, covering an area of 15,000 square metres), and the most spacious (5,724 square feet, or 532 square metres, per passenger). She also carries more passengers (2,620, plus a crew of 1,253) than any ship in history. No ship of this tonnage (150,000 tonnes gross, or three times as much as the *Titanic*) has ever been constructed.

Designing and building the ship was a little like constructing two liners in one: in terms of both its size and the hours it took to build, the *QM2* is the equivalent of two normal cruise ships. Europe's biggest dry dock was needed to accommodate it. Such excellence naturally had its cost—at $780 million, or 870 million Euros, the *QM2* is the world's most expensive passenger ship. But this was the price of producing a liner that was also the most robust, safest, and most environmentally friendly ever to sail the Atlantic.

Even before the *QM2* was built, the ship was already a legend, and she fascinated not only lovers of the sea and of ships but enthusiasts of magnificent industrial projects. For to build the liner that embodied all the superlatives—as she has often been described—imposes many constraints. Naval architects and engineers at Chantiers de l'Atlantique, the shipbuilders who constructed the ship at the Saint-Nazaire shipyard, had to produce sumptuous, original interior furnishings while also meeting the specific demands of this extraordinary vessel.

Born of a historic collaboration between the old and prestigious British steamship company Cunard and the Chantiers de l'Atlantique, *QM2* was the first Cunard ship in history to have been built in France. She is also the first transatlantic liner built by Chantiers de l'Atlantique since the celebrated *France* in 1962—a fact that made her construction, aside from her technical excellence, a great event and the subject of continuous interest.

As the months went by, the ship began her step-by-step metamorphosis—from the unfinished streamlined hull to the rounded curve of her still-grey bows, the appearance of her tiered rear decks, and, finally, to the brilliance of her red-and-black funnel. In the witnesses to these daily changes, both shipyard workers and enthusiasts, these daily changes created an impression of power along with a mixture of admiration and astonishment. Wasn't it amazing that such a huge ship could be so graceful? Beauty of form and technological excellence seemed to reinforce each other. The inseparability of these two elements, more than any motto, appears to have guided architects and workers throughout the vessel's construction. No doubt they were well aware that the *QM2* would not be a liner like any other. She would be immense, beautiful by design, and she would also be the first liner built in the twenty-first century, heralding a new way of travelling by sea and a new golden age of transatlantic sailing.

A Modern Transatlantic Liner

On 25 April 2004, the *Queen Elizabeth* 2, for the last three decades the only transatlantic liner in service, and the *Queen Mary* 2 sailed from the Port of New York for a coast-to-coast voyage, symbolising the handing over of the baton from one Cunard vessel to the other. Beyond her traditional three-month round-the-world cruise, the veteran ship will now be devoted to classic cruises in northern or southern Europe. The torch has been passed; *QM2*, the British company's new flagship, will be making the regular transatlantic crossings.

Running this route involves taking on a heavy set of responsibilities. A cruise liner puts into port every day, sailing only by night and in calm seas. The transatlantic liner takes on her passengers—travellers rather than tourists—whatever the weather, for six days' sailing in the North Atlantic, which can be furiously stormy in winter. The ship must be able to sail in rough weather, without slowing down or going off course. Thus, the seagoing qualities of *QM2* were the first consideration of her naval architects, Stephen Payne of Cunard in London and Jean-Jacques Gatepaille of Alstom Chantiers de l'Atlantique at Saint-Nazaire. While a cruise ship is above all a travelling hotel that disgorges her passengers for daily excursions, these architects had to account for the fact that a liner such as the *QM2*, carrying up to 3,090 passengers (2,620 under normal conditions) and a crew of 1,253, is a floating town. Life on board means that many public spaces are needed to play host to a far greater range of activities than are found on a cruise ship.

A fusion of liner and cruise ship—as intended by Carnival, owner of Cunard and thus the *QM2* as well—the *QM2* aims to be a highly capable seagoing vessel that can provide regular service between Southampton, England and New York and, at the same time, an extremely luxurious means of ocean transport that will attract passengers who want to cruise the sea of the Antilles or the Mediterranean. For the *QM2* will also drop anchor in the port of Rio, sail the Gulf of St. Lawrence and around the Cyclades, and explore Caribbean islands and Norwegian fjords.

This is why the vessel incorporates a feature typical of cruise ships: most cabins (almost 75 percent) have a balcony. Unlike those on Caribbean liners, these cabins are on the vessel's superstructure (which is usually devoted to public spaces such as restaurants or casinos) so that their balconies do not become swimming pools when the Atlantic waves cover the entire hull as high as Deck 2 or 3. On transatlantic liners in the last century, only first-class cabins were situated high up, while the crew and emigrants had to make do with the lower decks; on the *QM2*, all passengers enjoy these berths suspended between sky and sea.

Historical Continuity

As Stephen Payne, Cunard's naval architect, explains, "The balconies are the only visible concession to modernity, because I didn't want to impose anything that would have diluted that transatlantic experience. For example, there was no question of siting the public areas over the steering system, because no Cunarder has ever had such an arrangement." In a technical as well as an aesthetic sense, the *QE2* and the old transatlantic liners are the forbears of the prototype that is the *QM2*. The new ship incorporates the best features of both. Her unbroken internal thoroughfares, which allow passengers to travel the length of the ship, are modelled on the *Normandie* (1935). These obliged the architects to devise passages under the stalls in the two theatres, and tunnels through the mezzanine of the grand dining room so that passengers could go from the lobby to the discothèque without disturbing diners.

Deck 7, the 1,900-foot (580-metre) promenade running round the ship, is inspired by the *Rotterdam* (1959). As in the past, there is room for four people to walk abreast past the row of deckchairs that are an inseparable part of transatlantic liners. Parasols are no longer in fashion, but one might still come across the occasional gentleman in a Panama hat on this Mecca of socialising at sea. However, it not so much a matter of simply copying the past as of adapting it to today's tastes: now, the observation deck in the bow is covered, as are the bridge (inspired by the *QE2*) and the front of the ship's superstructure (worthy of the first *Queen Mary*)—in fact, both are completely enclosed.

The stern is a hybrid that draws on two Italian ships of the 1960s: the *Oceanic* and the *Eugenio C*. It is rounded above the waterline, which is both more attractive and reduces pitch in heavy weather, but vertical below it is on all modern cruise ships, which improves the hull's hydrodynamic properties.

Twelve Return Trips to the Moon

The need to cope with relentless bad weather in the North Atlantic creates a demand for technical specifications that are very different from those of a cruise ship. The *QM2* must make about fifteen return trips from Southampton, England to New York between April and December—a period during which the weather is often rough, especially around the equinox, when there are frequent storms with waves up to 50 feet (15 metres) high and winds of more than 60 knots (69 miles, or 110 kilometres) per hour. The *Queen Mary 2* had a rough baptism on her maiden crossing, when just after leaving the Isle of Wight she was hit by gusts of 70 knots (81 miles, or 130 kilometres) per hour! Even after the wind has died down, a heavy swell can still cause problems, exerting torsion on the ship's plates and creating tiny cracks—a common type of rapid wear that was considered during the vessel's design.

To withstand the force of the elements, the *QM2* has a hull built entirely of steel, with reinforced plates and a central spine that connects a structural frame to almost all the decks—a feature no longer found on Caribbean liners. With an expected fatigue life of forty years, without any extraordinary maintenance, the *QM2* will be able to sail a distance equivalent to twelve return trips to the moon.

Built to Take on the North Atlantic

Strength is not everything, however: a liner must be able to brave the elements with calm. The hull's hydrodynamics and the ship's power are the two factors that govern passenger comfort. The ocean swell must not be perceptible in the vessel's five swimming pools, and Deck 7, with its 360-degree promenade, must remain negotiable in all weather. This is why the design of the hull and stem were improved over what is found in cruise ships, with the prow being given its distinctive V shape. This pointed, streamlined bow, which unmistakably recalls the great transatlantic liners of the past, is not just for show. On the contrary, a slender hull accommodates fewer cabins than that of a squarer ship. It also complicates the interior layout, forcing naval architects to perform all manner of tricks to fit in all living and leisure facilities.

The first planetarium at sea, for instance, was a great challenge—built in the forward part of the hull, four decks high and topped with a 43-foot (13-metre) diameter dome. Certainly, atria the height of several decks—first seen on the *Sovereign of the Seas* (1987), also built at Saint-Nazaire—are now a common feature on cruise ships. But those are commonly situated in the centre of the ship; to make such an opening in the forward part, where the constraints are greater and there is minimum room for service ducts, involves a different level of space utilisation.

The slenderness of a hull—a challenge for designers but essential for good seaworthiness—is expressed as a block coefficient. Imagine that the ship is inside a rectangular block with height, width, and depth equal to those of the vessel itself. If the ship were to fill the block completely, its block coefficient would be 1. Cruise ships often have coefficients of 0.9; that of the *QM2* is just 0.58, thanks essentially to that slender hull. The *QM2* superstructure, too, looks nothing like those brick-shaped liners but rises instead in an elegant pyramid, thus placing the weight in the ship's centre and aiding her balance. To further reduce the effects of the swell, four stabilisers have been fitted to the hull. These fins, which weigh 70 tonnes and occupy a surface area of more than 160 square feet (15 square metres), can be deployed in thirty seconds and compensate for up to 90 percent of roll.

Finally, to achieve an average speed of 25 knots (on just 60 percent of available power), and a top speed of 30 knots (the same as the *Queen Elizabeth 2*), regardless of weather conditions or unfavourable currents, the *QM2*, with its high ratio of dead weight, must produce almost twice the power of a normal liner. The ability to travel at 28 or 30 knots could save a life—if, for example, the ship needed to be diverted to port rapidly—but it also allows the vessel to keep to her timetable.

Speed also comes from resistance-reducing equipment specially installed to streamline the ship's forward movement in the water, which can be subject to different types of drag. The casings that contain the propellers and the retraction of stabilisers both improve the hull's hydrodynamic properties. But increased speed depends above all on the bulbous bow—a hollow protuberance at the prow of the ship, level with the waterline, like an enormous false nose three decks high. Used on all vessels, whether oil tankers, container ships, or ocean liners, this feature produces a wave in opposition to those the ship creates with her forward movement through the water, which slow her down. If perfectly adapted to the hull shape, the bulbous bow allows an increase in speed of some 5 percent.

According to Jean-Jacques Gatepaille, one of the naval architects of the *QM2*, robustness of construction constantly took precedence over the ship's fittings and facilities. However, to look at the luxury and size of the cabins, one could have one's doubts!

150,000 Tonnes to Manoeuvre

The naval architects who designed the first liner of the twenty-first century did not aim to incorporate radically new technologies—unlike the builders of the *Normandie*, for example, which was unprecedented in its taut lines and improved hydrodynamics. The *Queen Mary 2* is evolutionary rather than revolutionary: its innovation lies in making use of all the available advanced shipbuilding technologies and adapting them on a gigantic scale. The real challenge was not so much reaching 30 knots as producing the power needed to propel the heaviest liner ever built (62,000 tonnes light, but 75,000 tonnes ready to sail).

The power needed to propel the 150,000 gross tonnes of the *QM2* is enormous, requiring an output unprecedented on a ship: 114 megawatts of electricity, or enough to light a city of 200,000—Southampton, say, or Saint-Nazaire three times over. The power plant responsible consists of four diesel engines situated in the bottom of the hull (because of their size and weight of 217 tonnes) and two gas turbines in the topsides, where air intakes function best. This approach by Chantiers de l'Atlantique is a classic one, but it comprises twice the power units normally fitted to a cruise ship. Although all this power is needed to reach 30 knots, the diesel generators alone are enough to maintain a cruising speed of 25 knots. When the *Queen Mary 2* is sailing in Alaskan waters or in other areas where there are strict environmental controls, she will comply with emissions regulations by using only the gas turbines, whose exhaust gases contains low levels of sulphur and nitric oxide.

The propulsion system is in keeping with this spirit of innovation that still carries the flavour of the past. Several years ago, Chantiers de l'Atlantique replaced the traditional propulsion system of the liners (a double propeller shaft and a rudder) with two "pods" (submerged assemblies, situated on the vault at the stern of the hull and able to rotate 360 degrees). This technology is not very far from that of outboard motors. Besides saving a considerable amount of space, this system vastly improves the manoeuvrability of the ship and almost completely reduces sounds and vibrations. On the *QM2*, it is not one pair but rather two that will be installed: two azimuthal and two one-directional. Driven by 3.2-megawatt thrusters, this system allows the *Queen Mary 2* to turn on the spot in port—a crucial facility if this giant of the seas is to moor at the Southampton berth of the *Queen Elizabeth 2*, where room is limited. And with due respect to the old ship's wheel and the nostalgia it inspires, all this is controlled simply by means of a joystick!

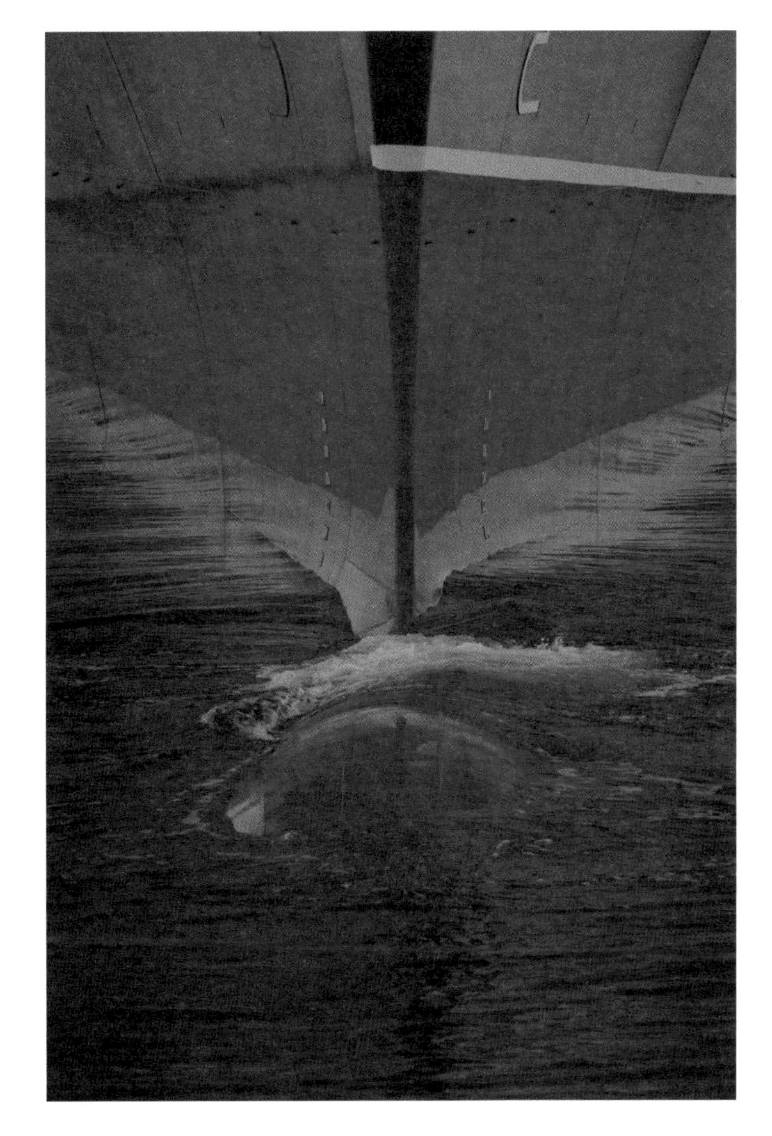

It was nevertheless a challenge to adapt this system to the giant proportions of the *QM2*. Built by Rolls Royce, and weighing in at 270 tonnes apiece, the four pod, are the biggest ever constructed and, at 21.5 megawatts each, the most powerful. They are controlled electrically rather than hydraulically, another innovation that allows more precise commands and minimises wear. The propellers are cast from stainless steel in place of the usual alloy of zinc and bronze. Their price is proportional, but they are guaranteed for life. In order to minimise vibration, their blades face forward, pulling the ship, in contrast to propellers facing aft, which propel the ship.

At the Click of a Mouse

High technology rules in the steering system, the ship's nerve centre. With the 148-foot (45-metre) beam, the control area could be laid out in accordance with the bridge crew operational management system, in which the control of navigation and safety systems is centralised on a series of screens. Radar, route, satellite navigation, various alarm systems, water and energy consumption, ballast transfer, and weather maps—all the ship's vital data are on constant display. With the click of a mouse, a window in the corner of a screen displays, in real time, the vantage point of any of the ship's 190 surveillance cameras. For the first time, all electric switchboards are sited at a single point, a small compartment accessed directly from the bridge. In case of a problem of any kind, the crew members on watch can immediately cut power from parts of the ship and can even close fire doors at the touch of a button.

The age of the *Titanic* is long past. Today, the greatest danger facing a transatlantic liner is not collision—even with an iceberg—but fire. For this reason, management of fire-fighting equipment is also centralised. A computerised system links 5,000 smoke detectors, 1,100 fire doors, and 8,350 "hi-fog" fire extinguishers fixed to ceilings. But Cunard has strengthened safety measures further, well beyond the legal requirements for passenger ships. Smoke extractors are a case in point. These are compulsory in atria, which can be expected to hold big crowds; but on the *Queen Mary 2*, all public spaces two floors or more high (such as the theatre, the planetarium, and the Britannia restaurant) are fitted with this system, which can remove all smoke in just ten minutes. This feature was especially appreciated by the U.S. Coast Guard, which paid several visits to Saint-Nazaire to approve safety systems.

A "Green" Liner

Icebergs, ocean currents, violent winds, and storms—the *QM2* fears nothing in her environment, the sea. It thus has a duty to respect it. The various environmental systems developed at Chantiers de l'Atlantique over the last twenty years or so were perfected on the *Millennium* (2000), which was a truly "green" liner. This concern with zero waste was built into the *QM2*, making Cunard's masterpiece one of the least polluting ships in the world.

It all begins on the ship's exterior, with antifouling paint on the hull that is not toxic to marine organisms, as required by international law. The air-conditioning system uses a cold-water network to minimise the amount of refrigerant gas on board, while the refrigeration system uses non-polluting gases that do not damage the ozone layer. Within the ship, there are two main concerns: to dump no waste at sea, and to recycle everything as much as possible. All liquids are treated, and solid waste is burned; non-combustible matter is stored on board and later unloaded when the ship reaches land. Waste water from bathrooms, kitchens, and laundries (some 10,000 table napkins are washed and ironed every day) are purified in a membrane bioreactor, a system that combines biological degradation with filtration. The recycled water is of drinking quality, and can be reused to wash decks, portholes, and laundry. Other liquid waste can be used in place of sea water to fill the ballast tanks. It is now known that when sea water is used as ballast, plants and animals are moved from one ecosystem and released into another, with the potential for seriously upsetting the environmental balance.

At all levels in its management and treatment of waste, therefore, the *QM2* leads the way, having been designed to standards far beyond those required by current European or U.S. legislation. As a zero waste ship, the ship's design also anticipates any possible tightening of international environmental protection regulations.

Combining tradition and modernity in this way demanded considerable technical innovation and flair. Although some of these systems and materials have already featured individually on other ships, they have never before been brought together in a single vessel. Neither have so many cabins been installed, nor has such a quantity of steel been worked at Chantiers de l'Atlantique. No other single project has employed so many engineers and workers. And never has such a large ship been built in such a short time: construction took just twenty-three months, while it took more than five years to build the *France* (1962), another legendary ship that, in its time, was the world's biggest transatlantic liner.

Such an undertaking was much more than a simple question of having the necessary know-how. It has only been made possible by people's willingness to invest their energy, challenge set attitudes, and exceed their achievements daily, all in the quest to travel further in the search for quality, in attention to detail, and in commitment to excellence in all the finishing touches. "Everything, absolutely everything, has been gone through with a fine-toothed comb," Jean-Rémy Villageois, *QM2* project manager at Chantiers de l'Atlantique, declared thoughtfully: "We tried to get close to perfection."

P 16

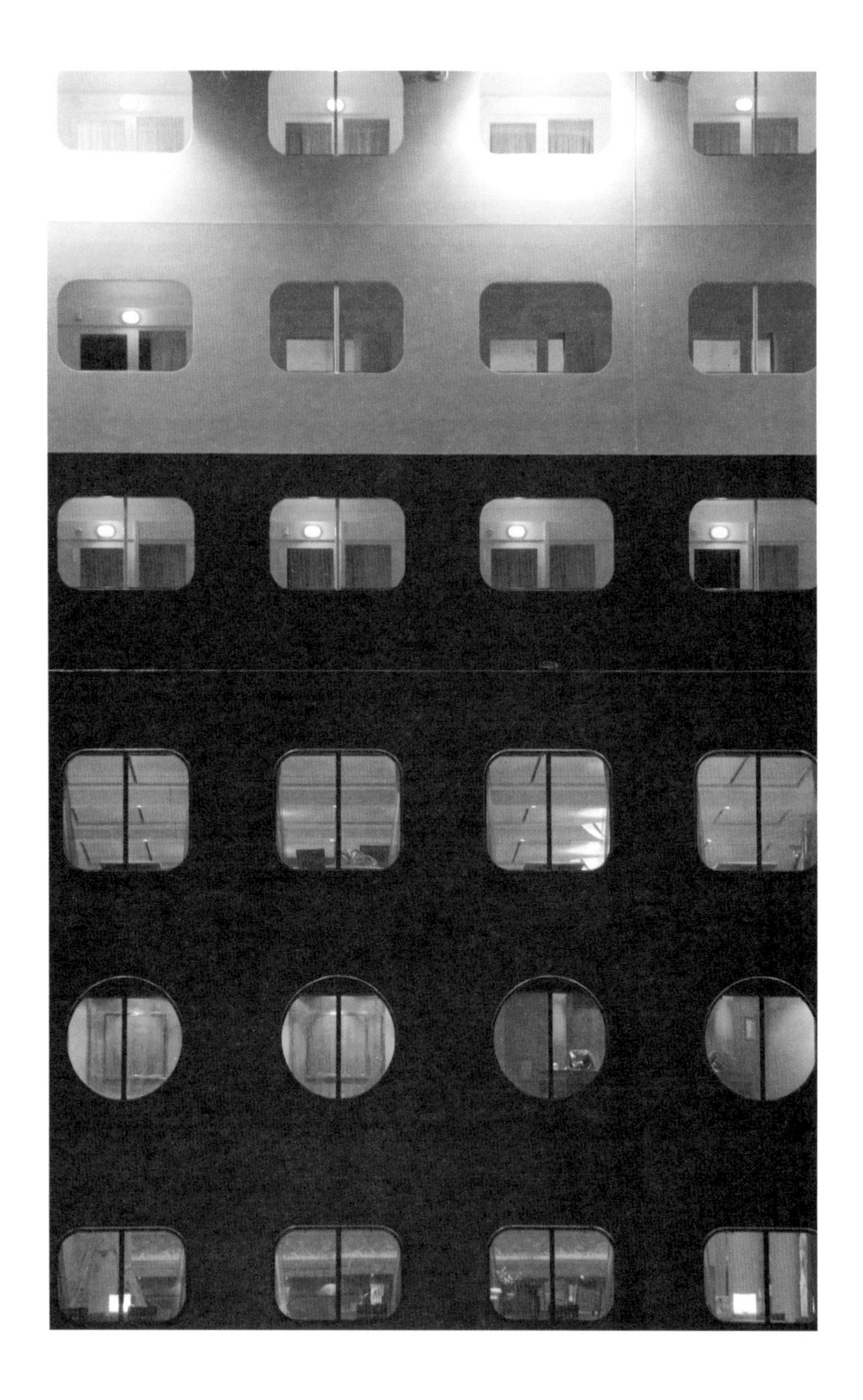

Que

THE CONSTRUCTION

THE BUILDING OF THE *QUEEN MARY 2* AT SAINT-NAZAIRE

Half a century was to pass before Cunard and Chantiers de l'Atlantique could come together. From its earliest days, Cunard Line had been faithful to the Scottish shipyards, especially that of John Brown on the Clyde, which in 1969 delivered what was then the latest transatlantic liner, the *Queen Elizabeth* 2. During this time, Chantiers de l'Atlantique built the ships for the Compagnie Générale Transatlantique at Saint-Nazaire, the last of these being the *France*, completed in 1962. For a long time, Cunard and "Transat," as the Compagnie Générale Transatlantique was known, were the two great rivals of the Atlantic, each vying with the other to launch the more beautiful liner or the faster. The two companies battled fiercely for the famous Blue Riband, awarded to the liner with the fastest Atlantic crossing from Bishop's Rock, off the English coast, to the Ambrose lightship in the Hudson estuary. During the 1930s, the prize changed hands several times between Transat's *Normandie* and Cunard's *Queen Mary*.

After the *France* stopped making its service run, the *Queen Elizabeth* 2 was the sole remaining ship offering a transatlantic crossing; Chantiers de l'Atlantique, meanwhile, was building one pleasure ship after another. Then, at the dawn of the twenty-first century, the two giants formed an alliance. Cunard Line and its mother company, Carnival, world leader in cruises, chose the world's premier cruise-ship builder to construct the first transatlantic liner in thirty years. She was to be a vessel more than five times longer than *Britannia*, the first Cunarder, which had been powered both by steam and by sail.

Chantiers de l'Atlantique

For a shipyard created by a Scottish engineer, who had mastered technology transfer before its time, this pact was a fitting return to roots. In 1861, the Pereire brothers signed a twenty-year contract with the French government to provide postal service on the Le Havre–New York and Saint-Nazaire–Panama routes. The brothers, who had founded the Compagnie Générale Transatlantique six years earlier, needed to build a fleet of vessels in France. They engaged a Scotsman, John Scott, to build and operate a shipyard at Penhoët, near Saint-Nazaire. Scott brought with him the techniques for building metal-hulled liners. Some fifteen British engineers supervised workers from the nearby Brière area, who were already skilled in building wooden-hulled vessels—in fact, the Loire estuary, especially around Nantes, had been a shipbuilding centre for centuries. The

Impératrice Eugénie, a liner with both paddles and sails, was delivered to Transat in 1865, the first of about 100 liners built at Saint-Nazaire. Although the Penhoët shipyard went bankrupt a year later, a new industry had been launched at the mouth of the Loire. In 1881, a law granting public subsidy to the construction of steamships boosted building activity, and several new shipyards were set up. Among these were Chantiers de la Loire, founded in 1882, and the Saint-Nazaire Shipyards and Workshops Limited Company (CP), owned by Transat and founded in 1900. The two firms merged in 1955, forming Chantiers de l'Atlantique. These shipyards brought the region wealth and employment, becoming part of a skilled maritime tradition that produced some of the most beautiful liners ever to sail the twentieth-century seas. The mythical vessels of the 1930s—such as the *Île de France* (1927) and the *Normandie* (1935), often considered the most beautiful transatlantic liner ever built—and the two *France* (1912 and 1962), will remain famous not only for their technical prowess but also for the luxury and refinement of their interiors.

In the 1960s, the construction of liners came to an abrupt halt. Ever since the fateful year of 1959, when more passengers crossed the Atlantic by air than by sea, the aircraft had become the preferred means for making the journey. Chantiers de l'Atlantique began to specialise in supertankers and in complex vessels such as methane tankers; in 1976, it merged with Alsthom (renamed Alstom in 1998).

But in the 1980s, ocean cruises became the fashion. Construction of passenger ships was revived, and the building of oil tankers shifted to yards in the Far East. The 1985 order for the *Sovereign of the Seas* ushered in a new era. Launched in 1987, the biggest passenger ship built in fifty years was also, at the time, the biggest liner in history. By the beginning of the third millennium, Europe's biggest shipyard was building more than a quarter of the world's cruise ships.

The Biggest Dry Dock in Europe

Cunard's choice of Chantiers de l'Atlantique as the builder of its first liner in more than thirty years was, for the shipyard, both a return to its roots and recognition of its expertise in running big projects.

One of Alstom's strengths was its success in surrounding a core of skilled people with a multitude of subcontractors and collaborators (who themselves awarded contracts to subcontractors). The Saint-Nazaire area's thriving maritime tradition had kept many small, local companies busy, experts in everything from welding to furnishing luxury dining rooms. Foreign specialists were also included, either due to their aptitude in a particular technology or because low added-value items were no longer produced by local companies: air-conditioning, for example, became the preserve of Italian and Indian companies.

10/03/2000

Signature of the letter of intent between Carnival and Alstom Marine

The gigantic scale of the *QM2* was reflected in the human resources mobilised to build her. The work of some 17,000 people (including 4,500 Alstom employees) had to be coordinated, who among them spoke twenty-six different languages and worked for 750 companies, whether suppliers or manufacturers. This mastery of coordination was a decisive factor in Cunard's choice of Saint-Nazaire, but it was not the only one. Geographical location—in a deep estuary and not on a river, like one of its competitors—played a part, but most important was the shipyard's dry dock. The biggest

6/11/2000

Signature of the contract

in Europe, the Saint-Nazaire dry dock was developed for building giant tankers. It is 1,640 feet (500 metres) long and features two assembly gantries in place of the one in other European yards, as well as the most up-to-date smelting and welding equipment.

The universally recognised technological excellence of Chantiers de l'Atlantique could not help but win over Cunard, a company that had itself so often been at the forefront. As early as 1848, the ship company was equipping its vessels with the first light signalling system, now used on all boats (a white light at the masthead, a green one to starboard, and a red one to port). Innovation has also been one of the strong points of Chantiers de l'Atlantique, from the first "ecological" sail- and steam-powered liners of the Millennium series (2000–2002) to the revolutionary ventilation process invented for the *Normandie*, to the new pod-based propulsion system fitted on all new-generation cruise ships.

But if three key men devoted to the tradition of the great transatlantic liners had not met, would such objective criteria alone have been enough? Stephen Payne and Jean-Jacques Gatepaille, the two naval architects, and Jean-Rémy Villageois, project manager on the *QM2*, worked together hand in glove. Driven by a common desire to produce something beautiful, they revisited a traditional theme, drawing on the best from the past while building for the future: a ship of the line that was also the most comfortable leisure cruiser, combining British elegance with leading-edge technologies. After the Concorde and the Channel tunnel, the *QM2* was another Franco-British collaboration—"the one which will be most successful!" as Stephen Payne declared, smiling.

THE MAIN STAGES OF CONSTRUCTION

A Paper Boat: Preliminary Studies (December 2000–December 2001)

The ship first saw the light on paper and on the computer screen. As with trains and aircraft—such as the Airbus A380, the largest civilian aircraft ever built, whose front and central fuselages were also assembled at Saint-Nazaire—the preliminary study is one of the most important phases in construction. The conception of the *QM2* thus began long before Pamela Conover, Cunard's president, cut its first steel plate (a rectangular section measuring 8 by 11 inches [20 by 30 centimetres] and weighing 10 pounds [4.5 kilograms]) on 16 January 2002. That act marked the start of a race against the clock: 700 days and 8 million man-hours later, the *QM2* was to leave Saint-Nazaire for her home port, Southampton. Indeed, the ship's conception began even before the contract was signed on 6 November 2000. In fact, after the naval architect at Chantiers de l'Atlantique had given his views as to the feasibility and cost calculations of Cunard's project, a dozen design engineers fine-tuned his figures to come up with a binding offer (consisting of a price and plans) for the ship company, which responded with a letter of intent stating it wanted to go ahead. Its codename: G32—and the source of the name of *QM2*'s discotheque!

At the end of 2000, some fifty people were gathered together from all Alstom Marine's various areas of expertise. For a year they looked closely at the ship company's plans and technical specifications, checking and—where applicable—changing them. The question was no longer whether Chantiers de l'Atlantique could build the world's biggest liner; the question was how it would build it. This involved calculating the strength of individual materials as well as planning the assembly of the ship and running trials in a testing tank using a 60-foot (18-metre) model. How best to optimise the space needed to accommodate all the cabling, water pipes, air ducts, and wiring? Did access routes (stairs, gangways, and emergency exits) comply with international regulations (SOLAS and OMI)? Which propulsion system best met the ship company's fuel consumption needs? Was the available power sufficient? Were Cunard's wishes regarding certain interior furnishings compatible with safety regulations? All these questions produced lively—sometimes heated—debate among the engineering and design departments of Chantiers de l'Atlantique and Cunard. This phase of intense negotiations richly benefited both sides. A million hours were spent on planning, engineering, and design, and Alstom examined some 6,000 plans, of which almost 1,000 were submitted to naval architect Stephen Payne for approval.

Technical suitability aside, aesthetic criteria were often the deciding factor. For example, the highly streamlined front section, a hallmark of the *QM2*, needed three times as much work as those of ordinary liners—including two months of 3D computer imaging (using a technique developed specifically for the *QM2*) simply for the top row of windows! Although historical research and attention to attractive design were connecting threads throughout the design phase, the engineering was firmly based on practical needs within the limits of what was possible. As Jean-Rémy Villageois explained, "It was a magical time: there was a constant back and forth between those responsible for the ship's functions (propulsion, energy generation, interior circulation, controls) and the engineers who were working on the layout, dealing with space and volumes and fitting the functions within the ship. The challenge was reconciling these, and meeting the needs of each—for example, so that the architects designing the interior should not forget to leave space for ventilation ducts. This way of working autonomously and in parallel is at the heart of the effectiveness of Chantiers de l'Atlantique." As soon as a plan was finalised, the multidisciplinary team passed it on to the in-house engineers (all specialised in their own fields, such as public spaces or propulsion). They in turn followed their part of it to the end, submitting orders to suppliers so that everything was ready in time as construction proceeded. At the end of the engineering and design stage, all decisions had been definitively confirmed and the ship could be built, in accordance with the highly specific timetable and specifications drawn up especially for a vessel of this enormous size.

February 2001

Successful trials on models in the testing tank

A Steel Monster: Machining the Plates (January 2002–January 2003)

The volume of steel needed to build the hull speaks for itself: 52,000 tonnes, cut up into 300,000 sections held together by 930 miles (1,500 kilometres) of welds. Never had so much steel passed through the preassembly workshops of Chantiers de l'Atlantique. And therein lay one of the challenges in building the *QM2*: coordinating the hundreds of workers who had to work in parallel. A total of 1,500 people, about half of them from outside the shipyard, were to build the ship's metal shell (hull and superstructure) in less than fourteen months—a feat of organisation. The yard buzzed with this swarm of people in blue overalls, who pedalled around on hundreds of yellow bicycles provided to help them move quickly from one site to another. Several other ships were also under construction at the time; those lucky enough to be working on the one known as "the Queen" were already proud of having taken part in the "birth of a legend."

16/01/2002

Cutting of the first plate

Engineering and design was not yet complete when the plates were delivered by rail from Belgium and Poland. Immediately, they were cleaned and painted for identification. "Ordinary" plates—measuring 23 or 28 millimetres thick (instead of the 20 millimetres usual on Caribbean liners), or even 30 millimetres at the superstructure joint on Deck 7—were painted grey, while the more elastic (and therefore stronger) plates were painted mauve. The latter were to be used especially in the upper parts of the ship, where deformation could sometimes be as much as 20 inches (50 centimetres). Then the plates were machined—that is, cut into specifically shaped pieces or joined together to form sheets, or two-dimensional elements. Most of the sheets were later made into three-dimensional panels weighing an average of 50 tonnes, which were in turn welded together to form blocks weighing in excess of 700 tonnes. All this was carried out in the shipyard's historic heart, even though the techniques had developed immensely since the nineteenth century. Those who work there are still called *charpentiers fer* (fabricators or platers) along with welders, boilermakers, and straighteners, but today the metal is cut using plasma cutters or lasers, and welding is done continuously using inert gas and no longer electrodes. Today, workers are more likely to be sitting at the control screen of a machine that automatically cuts 80 percent of plates than be up to their elbows in grease. There has also been another minor revolution in this world of iron and fire: the astonished visitor might well glimpse, behind the shower of sparks of a welding machine, the face of a woman—one out of 800 welders was female, but a total of fifty-two women worked on the *QM2*.

There remain, however, some bastions of craftsmanship, where certain complex pieces need to be made almost entirely by hand. In the "180-tonne workshop," for instance, some 300 people worked together to build one panel every five weeks, whereas the "flat-panel" workshop, the most mechanised, produced panels at the rate of one a week. The "180-tonne workshop" was where complex components and large panels that could not be made automatically were painstakingly assembled, such as ballast tanks, the stem, and the stern panel. Such unique pieces are the pride of boilermakers, whose skills have been handed down over generations. The ship's funnel and the front of her superstructure are thus symbolic in two ways: they are unmistakable Cunard features as well as a justifiable source of pride for Chantiers de l'Atlantique workers. You need only picture a round funnel, 40 feet (12 metres) high, hand-shaped from a single fine sheet of metal so that no weld is discernible—perfection itself!

A Meccano Game: Assembly of the Blocks (July 2002–February 2003)

04/07/2002

Placing of the first block on stocks

With the panels taking shape in the workshops, the first blocks were placed along the stocks and fitted with casings, cabling, small motors, and air-conditioning equipment. Performed in parallel, this work saved time and ensured that there would be no need to make an opening in an awkward place later on.

On 4 July 2002, six months after the first plate was cut, the first of the ship's ninety-four blocks was placed on the stocks. Topped with wooden blocks, the 330 steel posts were able to bear a weight of 111,300 tonnes (though the *QM2* weighs "only" 62,000 tonnes) and kept the bottom of the dry dock from sinking. The laying of Block 502, the starboard engine bay, inaugurated the assembly phase—the most impressive stage of the ship's construction—in a ceremony accompanied by the Celtic strains of the Bagad de Lann Bihoué naval band. Captain Ron Warwick jokingly asked the crane operator to lay the first block of "his" ship. Captain Warwick, who had been officially appointed first officer of the *QM2* by Cunard's president a few minutes before the ceremony, comes from a seafaring family: his father, Commodore W. E. Warwick, was the first captain of the *Queen Elizabeth 2*, a post in which his son succeeded him in 1990.

27/08/2002

Installation of the diesel motors

The date of 4 July had not been chosen at random: it is Independence Day in the United States, Carnival's home country, and also Cunard's birthday. Exactly 162 years earlier, on 4 July 1840, the company's first ship, the *Britannia*, left Liverpool on her maiden voyage to Boston. On this historic day, the ship company and the shipyard observed a tradition dating from the ancient Greeks: coins were welded to the bottom of the hull to bring good luck to the ship as well as to her builder, owner, and passengers. A £5 coin minted in commemoration of the fiftieth anniversary of the queen's coronation symbolised the United Kingdom, while a gold coin bearing the image of Louis Philippe symbolised France, where the ship was built.

Next day, the "cathedrals" of Saint-Nazaire began their performance. These gigantic gantries are the symbol of the town, and the first structures to come into view whether it is approached by sea or by land. Manoeuvred by just one person who works the controls in a suspended cabin, they attach one to another in just thirty minutes and are accurate to the millimetre.

Like a gigantic Meccano set, the steel blocks gradually took on the shape of a vessel, starting with the bottom of the hull. By the end of August, all the blocks at the bottom had been assembled. This space accommodated the diesel engines, which, together with the gas turbines, would generate all the electricity the vessel needed to drive her propellers and for the on-board power supply. The first block above the waterline was laid at the end of September. Two months later, the vessel's interior, in the form of the aluminium frame and the dome of the planetarium, had begun to be fitted—unusual at this stage in a ship's construction. The planetarium, however, rises through four decks to a height of 26 feet (8 metres), with a diameter of 43 feet (13 metres), and had to be installed before the upper decks were put in place.

By this stage, the steel shell already looked like a ship, 721 feet (220 metres) long with seven decks. It was time to float her for the first time. She was moved forward a hundred feet or so toward the deep part of the stocks, vacating her original space for the construction of another ship. Assembly continued with the placing of more blocks, and a number of milestones were passed: the attachment of the bulbous bow, welded to the front of the hull like a gigantic spur, and the fixing of Block 509, the last of the lower part of the hull, on 16 January 2003. From this point on, the ship would grow upward. Within the space of a few days, between 27 January and 4 February 2003, the three blocks were laid that best define the identity of the *QM2*: the last block of the stem, a magnificent V shape, not only bore the ship's name but bestowed her elegant, streamlined bows; the last block of the stern, the rounded rear quarter-deck seen on all transatlantic liners and bearing the name "Southampton," her home port; and finally the wheelhouse—at 630 tonnes, the heaviest block, and the widest at 148 feet (45 metres). Just eight more months were scheduled for the completion the world's biggest liner.

In March 2003 the ship, like a vast multilayered cake of steel plates, was ready to take to the water and be towed to the fitting-out dock, a few hundred metres downstream. This was the first moment of truth, and the first great thrill for the 5 A.M. crowd that gathered at the entrance to the port of Saint-Nazaire. The ship's plates were still unpainted, and her superstructure still ghostlike, but already she floated proudly on the water. And yet something was lacking. . .the funnel's top section, which was not yet in place. This last block would not be laid until 4 April 2003, in the fitting-out dock. As the funnel would have taken the vessel to her full height of 236 feet (72 metres), she would have been too tall to cross between the assembly gantries—though not to pass under New York's Verrazano Narrows Bridge, to whose clearance the ship's height had been tailored. Depending on the tide and the expansion of the metal bridge in summer, the clearance ranges from 13.5 to 25.6 feet (4.1 to 7.8 metres) between the bridge and the vessel's funnel, painted in Cunard's colours of red and black.

Fitting Out (March–December 2003)

No sooner had *QM2* taken to the sea than she was back again, in Dock C. This is where she would be transformed into a true floating village: an independent island that must generate its own electricity, recycle its waste, and look after the needs and desires of its 4,000 or so residents. Now,

26/11/2002
Installation of the dome of the planetarium

01/12/2002
Transfer to deep stocks

14/12/2002
Installation of the bulbous bow

27/01/2003
Installation of the stem

1/02/2003
Installation of the rear quarter-deck

4/02/2003
Installation of the wheelhouse

13/03/2003
Installation of the funnel

21/03/2003
Transfer to the fitting-out dock

May 2003
Half of the 2,017 cabins are installed

6/06/2003
Installation of the first pod

25/09/2003
First sea trials

31/10/2003
Waterline is painted in white; finishing paint touches to the hull

7/11/2003
Second sea trials

closer to the port and to the centre of Saint-Nazaire, the *QM2* became a destination in her own right, attracting tens of thousands of visitors come to witness the birth of the biggest "château of the Loire," as the mayor of Saint-Nazaire likes to call the liners that leave the estuary. From a distance, some of these visitors could watch the fitting of the pods, the first of which was installed under the hull on 6 June 2003 in an especially delicate operation. Two 700-tonne cranes lifted, swivelled, and lowered to the dock's bottom the 270-tonne pod, which had to remain horizontal throughout the procedure.

Although all the elements supporting pipework, electric-cable routing, ventilation, and so forth had been installed gradually as the blocks were put in place, as had most thermal insulation, soundproofing, and fire protection, the bulk of the fitting-out still remained to be done during the eight months the vessel would be in the dock. This meant installing the prefabricated cabins and kitchen equipment, linking up all pipework, completing the control and safety systems, painting the hull, putting decorations and works of art in public areas, lining the walls, and putting furniture in place.

By this time the ship looked like a great beehive, where 3,000 people could work at the same time, generally in two eight-hour shifts. Employees from dozens of different companies managed to work together thanks to the coordination arranged by Chantiers de l'Atlantique, which needed to ensure that all could work efficiently and in complete safety. The planning headache can be imagined. Had it not been for the crying of the gulls, one might have imagined oneself in a vast hotel under construction, where everything is made to measure. Curtains, carpets, chairs, original lithographs and sculptures, crockery, and so forth had all been designed and made specially for the *QM2*. And, as in haute couture, apart from their rarity, it was the quality of items often made on a small scale that stood out, as in the case of the smooth ceilings, cornices, domes, and soffits made of staff, a mixture of plaster with fibreglass or hemp that allows lighter applications and continuous surfaces without joints, as in an old house. Chantiers de l'Atlantique is the only shipyard in Europe that still employs people skilled in this technique, which it developed and modernised for the *QM2*, so that the vessel now boasts the only staff partitions.

The main task for Chantiers de l'Atlantique was to design and construct the steel hull, not to mention coordinate the hundreds of subcontractors. By contrast, the fittings are the realm of the shipyard's collaborators, companies which specialise in everything from swimming pools to casinos to decorative panels. Many firms in the Saint-Nazaire region are expert in fitting liners, such as Ateliers Normands of Nantes, which already worked on the *France*, and which here built the Winter Garden, with its hand-painted ceiling, and the four royal suites.

The first trials also took place during this period. Pipework was brought up to full pressure to test for leaks, the main electric switchboard was brought up to full power, lighting was tested, and the various safety systems (smoke detectors, extinguisher systems, and warning systems) were given a trial run, as was the power-generation unit. About 90 percent of the testing was done in the dock, though this would have to be confirmed by trials at sea, as specified in the contract.

And Now the Real Thing: Sea Trials

The carpets had not even been laid yet when, on 25 September 2003, the first sea trials took place. For the vessel's first outing, a crowd of 40,000 gathered on land and at sea. Under a swarm of helicopters, naval patrols kept small craft away from the liner. When the five tugboats that had guided the *QM2* along the fairway slipped their towropes and the captain blew the whistle (which can be heard ten miles away), it was greeted by an ovation.

A total of 450 people—engineers, technicians, ship company and insurance company representatives, and crew—spent four days on board as the ship shuttled between the islands of Belle-Île and L'Île d'Yeu. The tests included tuning machinery (power units and thrusters), dropping the anchors, testing the transverse thrusters and stabilisers, ensuring manoeuvrability (emergency stop, zigzagging, tight turns), checking navigation equipment (radar, automatic pilot, and radio), and testing acoustic and vibration damping. This was the moment of truth for the engineers, who now saw concrete confirmation of their theoretical calculations. Everyone heaved a sigh of relief when the level of vibration was judged compliant with the stringent standards—not only that, but the ship was also found to be extremely quiet. Certainly the countless drafts, trials on models and, during the building phase, simulations of propeller vibration had all predicted an acceptable noise level, but here was confirmation: the passengers would be able to sleep soundly. And they would not even be aware of acceleration, the shipyard's engineers asserted, when the vessel went from a standstill to 30 knots in ten minutes. Six weeks later, the second set of sea trials confirmed that all the levels of performance demanded by the contract and by regulations had been met. The most spectacular test of all, the "crash stop" (at top speed, 30 knots—about 34 miles, or 55.5 kilometres per hour—propellers are reversed, and the ship is brought to a halt within minutes) was held in a general atmosphere of celebration. The engineers were jubilant: the *Queen Mary 2* had exceeded their wildest hopes.

Fair Wind!

On Monday, 22 December 2003, the queen of the seas bade farewell to all who had lived and breathed for her over the last three years. At 9:45 A.M., an announcement echoed over the ship's decks: "The vessel is no longer ours!" The final signing for the purchase by Carnival had just taken place. All on board—shipyard employees and subcontractors making last-minute checks, journalists, and even bystanders (36,000 people had visited the floating palace on the weekend)—felt a tug at the heart. A quarter of an hour later the loudspeakers announced, this time in English, that all safety systems had been transferred to Cunard, which from now on was wholly responsible for the ship. Now it was the turn of the crew's and British service staff's hearts to beat fast!

Two hours later, all that remained was the change of flag, a formality but at the same time the most symbolic moment of the delivery. The ceremony was relayed to a video screen in the planetarium, where some 600 guests waited in silence after listening to the ministers of industry and employment praise the work of Chantiers de l'Atlantique.

Upon the order of Patrick Boissier, the shipyard's chief executive, the French flag and the Alstom pennant were lowered. The British flag and the Cunard pennant, bearing a golden lion

22/12/2003

Delivery to Cunard and departure from Saint-Nazaire for Southampton

on a red background, were then raised to the masthead to the strains of *God Save the Queen*.

After a lunch served in the Britannia restaurant to 600 distinguished guests—a sort of dress rehearsal for the cooks, waiters, and maîtres d'hôtel—Micky Arison, Carnival's chief executive officer, along with Pamela Conover, Carnival's president, and Patrick Boissier climbed aboard *Pêcheur d'images*, the catamaran belonging to Philip Plisson, to accompany the *Queen Mary* 2 out of her berth. Still in mourning over the tragic accident a month earlier, in which fifteen private visitors were killed, the town could not celebrate the end of this adventure with a light heart, but its pride remained undiminished. Tens of thousands of people braved the icy cold and thronged the coast to watch the first transatlantic liner of the twenty-first century set forth.

When Captain Warwick sounded the four whistles—one of which had originally belonged to the first *Queen Mary*—and the tugboats and navy vessels sprayed water into the air in her honour, the perfect formation of the eight aircraft of the Patrouille de France (French aerobatics formation) saluted her departure in a trail of red, white, and blue. The crew was on deck to wave to the crowd, which could see the banner draped on the ship's side: "Thank you Saint-Nazaire." Many of those present remembered the day the *France* left the harbour. Forty years later, they again experienced the same emotion: that of a dream come true.

LIFE ON BOARD

LIFE ON BOARD BETWEEN TWO CONTINENTS

Embarking on the *QM2* entails, first and foremost, a desire to cross the Atlantic from Southampton to New York. It means wanting to leave behind land and the hurly-burly of daily life, and savour the hours as they pass—each like the other and yet always different, like the sea itself. It means wanting to live to a different rhythm, relaxed and sociable, in the tradition of the Cunarders who, every year without fail since 1840, have set forth to conquer the North Atlantic. Already, the new liner's first passengers have made their preferences clear. The Atlantic crossing has proved so popular that some twenty-six are planned for 2005, or more than twice as many as in the ship's inaugural year. Cunard has not offered so many in nearly twenty years.

An Enchanted World

A crossing offers an unparalleled magic, the daily experience of another world. The *QM2* takes after a long line of Cunarders, ships that are instantly recognisable by their charcoal-grey, almost black, hulls and their red funnels striped in black. "Elegant, eclectic, and imposing," as Stephen Payne described her, the *QM2* is equally so within; the Cunard style, all pastel colours, is visible in the smallest detail: dark wood fittings; thick carpeting (more than 2.5 million square feet—235,000 square metres—or ten times the area of the Olympic stadium in Athens); teak decks; soft lighting; glass panels; warm hues of yellow, brown, red, and beige; glass and bronze statues; bas-reliefs; and glass decorated with gold or silver leaf—original art works by artists of all nationalities—create an atmosphere of British elegance far removed from the garish decoration of some cruise ships.

Those familiar with the *Queen Elizabeth 2* will feel at home, so closely do the public areas respect the transatlantic tradition. There is a running track, kennels for pets, an open-air observation deck below the bridge, the great Britannia dining room, and the gigantic Queen's Room, which is a ballroom in the evening and hosts the captain's afternoon tea and cocktails during the day. The Golden Lion continues a tradition begun in 1911 with the *Laconia*, the first ship in which the smoking room was furnished to resemble an old English pub, with leaded windows and a fireplace.

But even though she shares with them some of her furnishings and the Art Deco style, the *QM2* is no mere replica of earlier Cunarders—far from it. Her saloons and gangways instantly give the feeling of being exceptionally spacious. Just how spacious can be seen from the daily experience of her captain. Captain Warwick could reach the stern of the *Queen Elizabeth 2* from his cabin in the bows in twenty minutes, but his journey takes four times as long on the *QM2*!

A ceiling height of nearly 15 feet (4.5 metres), rather than the usual 12 or so (3.8 metres) on Decks 2 and 3, and the ability to open up the public spaces to encompass the entire 135-foot (41-metre) width of the vessel, have allowed the decorators to let their imagination run wild. The grand lobby is an atrium 60 feet (18 metres) high, and the largest restaurant at sea (1,350 places) is served by a double staircase, inviting sweeping descents to the captain's table at formal dinners—not to mention the nine other restaurants, fourteen bars and clubs, a theatre with more than 1,000 seats, five swimming pools, a casino, eight Jacuzzis, a 20,000-square-foot (1,860-square-metre) balneotherapy (a spa method using water) area, a hospital with operating theatre, and a library.

The décor itself is deliberately designed to re-create the charm of the past. The interior design firm Tillberg Design specialises in liners, having notably renovated the *Queen Elizabeth* 2 and designed the interior of the next Cunarder, the *Queen Victoria*. Rather than making a pastiche, it has created a contemporary interpretation of the décor of the liners of the Golden Age of the 1920s and 1930s. Part tribute and part nostalgia, the décor is inspired by the first *Queen Mary*, the *Normandie*, and by the "Odeon style." This last takes its name from those British cinemas with rounded façades topped by neon-lit towers, rather like strange would-be ocean liners with a hint of Eltham Palace in London, a veritable temple of Art Deco. In the centre of the ship, the grand lobby epitomizes this style: the double staircase decorated with engraved glass panels, the columns and cornices in staff, the grand piano surrounded by armchairs and low tables of contemporary Italian design with 1930s overtones, the ebony woodwork, panoramic lifts serving six levels of this majestic entrance, the more-than-500-square-foot (7 metres by 7 metres square) bronze bas-relief depicting the ship, right down to the typeface used for signs, which was designed at the time of the first *Queen Mary*. Everything conspires to bear the traveller who boards the *QM2* back to an enchanted time.

A Thousand Diversions

After the décor has been fully appreciated, it is time to settle down into a stress-free daily routine and enjoy the transatlantic experience. The days can be used to their fullest by exploring the ship and her many attractions (most of which are on Decks 2, 3, and 7), experiencing the sea, and taking part in cultural and sporting activities as a discerning amateur. On the *QM2* there are no games or competitions such as those found in holiday camps. Rather, conferences are held during the morning, and productions worthy of the West End are performed during the evening, notably by students of the Royal Academy of Dramatic Art, who take it in shifts to perform all the year round—a chance to spot tomorrow's stars.

Today, as in times before, meeting new people is one of the greatest pleasures of a transatlantic voyage. People recognise each other, start to extend greetings, and soon ties are formed, thanks to natural affinity or shared interests. It is easy to find kindred spirits among the joggers who run the longest training track at sea, the lovers of thalassotherapy (a technique using seawater and other ocean products to restore and invigorate), voracious readers in the library (which houses 8,000 volumes), or students of the "College at Sea" (with courses in computers, seamanship, history of art, wine, languages, theatre, and photography)—all complemented by a new programme of conferences in partnership with Oxford University. The promenade deck continues in this tradition. Whether you are stretched out on a teak deckchair reading a book, or strolling along gazing at the ocean horizon, it is a place conducive to meetings, which could then be continued within, where the mood takes you. There is the panoramic Commodore Club at the forward end of Deck 9, which harks back to the first-class observation saloon of the *Queen Mary* and where you can enjoy aperitifs to the sound of a jazz group; there are the club armchairs of the Cigar Lounge; and there is the Atlantic Room, an enclosed space in the middle of the observation point on Deck 11 (perfect for a wedding)—all are on a human scale and conducive to intimate conversation.

For an even more intimate atmosphere, there are always the cabins, which are comfortable, soundproofed cocoons. The lucky occupants of the duplex cabins—which, combined with the penthouses, offer more than 8,000 square feet (770 square metres) of private apartment—and of the 172 suites, can easily entertain in their own quarters, thanks to the private saloons and bars. The majority of passengers, who occupy any of the 782 deluxe or premium 300-square-foot (26-square-metre) cabins with balcony, may prefer to meet in the champagne bar, wine bar, or perhaps in the restaurant of Todd English, the famous American chef and convert to Mediterranean cuisine, where dinner can be eaten on the terrace of Deck 8.

Days at Sea

Eating is one of the chief activities on board a liner. No fewer than five meals and snacks per day are provided for all cabins, on top of which there are the delights of room service, available round the clock. During ocean crossings, life at sea follows the rhythms of mealtimes. Breakfast and lunch are taken at will, either in the traditional restaurants or in the King's Court buffets, with their 478 seats. Between these two meals it is customary to go for a walk, even play some sport, and to attend a conference. No longer are ladies expected to delay their arrival on deck until 10 A.M., to allow time for cleaning and for gentlemen to take their exercise. Today, the Canyon Ranch health centre offers the whole range of balneotherapy treatment as well as a gym boasting the most modern equipment, a far-removed descendant of the mechanotherapy rooms of the first transatlantic liners, with their vaulting horses and rowing machines. However, shuffleboard, a game played on British liners since the nineteenth century, is still available on the top deck alongside another reminder of the past, the giant chessboard. The various deck games are complemented by sports facilities, which can be found as high as 200 feet (60 metres) above the water line: a golf simulator, basketball court, putting green, mini-tennis, ping-pong, and a gymnastics and weight-training room with sea views.

What to do after lunch? How about a visit to the Queen's Room for bingo? Or perhaps it's time to write your diary in the library or the winter gardens, successors to the correspondence rooms that have now disappeared from liners. There are the gallery-museums of the history of Cunard to discover, armed with an audio-guide, and there are the sun decks, swimming pools, and Jacuzzis. Do not be too tempted by the barbecue in the Boardwalk Café, next to the big swimming pool with the retractable roof, for soon it will be time for high tea, served in the best English tradition. In late afternoon, why not visit the art gallery, with its original paintings by Picasso, Miró, and Chagall (for sale), sip a cocktail in the Queen's Room while each passenger has a photograph taken shaking hands with the captain, or hunt through the Mayfair Shops gallery—with its eight shops, covering more than 5,000 square feet (almost 500 square metres) and including Hermès and Dunhill—for a little something that will make all the difference at tonight's grand dinner. Soon it is 6 P.M. and nearly time to dress: on the *QM2*, evening gowns and dinner jackets (which can be hired on board) are compulsory on two evenings every crossing. Unaccompanied women need have no fears: there are eleven gentlemen on board available to accompany them to the grand ball.

After enjoying a drink and nibbling a few canapés in one of the ship's many bars, it is time to taste the delicacies concocted by Cunard's traditional chef—who has thirty years' service on the *Queen Elizabeth 2*—or the new recipes created by Daniel Boulud, the French chef who has settled in New York, or from the spa dishes recommended by Canyon Ranch. You can choose between elegant dinners in the Britannia or less formal meals in King's Court, which metamorphoses every afternoon into an Asian restaurant. There is an Italian trattoria open at all hours, an English restaurant, and even a high-tech restaurant where you can watch, on a giant screen, your dish being prepared by guest chefs who make cooking into a living art. You will not be surprised to learn that the *QM2* is the world's biggest consumer of caviar, and that some 61,000 pounds (28,000 kilograms) of lobster are served on board in the course of a year! Nor will it astonish you to hear that the biggest wine cellar at sea, boasting 343 types, sells almost 230,000 bottles and brews 60,000 pints of beer every year, and that 1,000 bottles of champagne are drunk every day. For an ordinary Atlantic crossing, the *QM2* takes on 14,000 dozen eggs, 8,500 pounds (3,850 kilograms) of beef tenderloin, 3,500 pounds (1,600 kilograms) of sole, and 7,700 pounds (3,500 kilograms) of prawns.

After dinner, some will try their luck in the casino, inspired by Monte Carlo, which offers 122 gambling machines and 11 tables. Others will visit the open-air cinema—another *QM2* innovation—with screenings on appropriate evenings on the upper deck. But most passengers will spend the evening at the Royal Court Theatre, named after the famous theatre in Sloane Square, London. Equipped with a hydraulically operated stage and the latest sound and light technology, it stages plays and musicals created specially for the *QM2*. Romantic souls may prefer to take refuge in the cabaretlike atmosphere of the Illuminations saloon, to sip a cocktail under the starry vault of the planetarium. This feature, never seen before on a ship, shows the constellations, after which you can go out on deck and admire the real thing, unspoiled by any light pollution. After a final drink in the Chart Room, ringing to the nostalgic airs of a cabaret singer, or in the G32 discothèque, worthy of Captain Nemo's *Nautilus* with its exposed metal structures, it is time to retire to your quarters—but not before calling on the "pillow steward," who offers nine different types, from the firmest to the softest!

A Town on the Atlantic

The *QM2* is not so much a floating palace as an entire town. As in a town on land, people eat, drink, sleep, cultivate and entertain themselves, play sports, shop, visit the dentist or hairdresser, receive guests, study, undergo medical treatment, and even work or keep track of their business affairs from a distance. Each cabin has a direct telephone line (connected via the Immarsat satellite) and interactive television in English, German, and French which, apart from giving details of each day's activities, can be used to reserve excursions on land or yoga classes, to see and buy photographs, and to access the Internet or read e-mail. There is also the business centre, sited in the "ConneXions" area; the education centre, which comprises seven classrooms or conference rooms; and fifty terminals connected to the Internet.

The real workers in this town at sea, those that allow it to function and make it both pleasant and autonomous, are the army of cooks, chambermaids, musicians, naval officers, waiters, masseurs, comedians, mechanics, laundresses, and attendants. In all, a crew of 1,253 people looks after the comfort, safety, and well-being of some 2,620 passengers. From the private steward of the luxury suites, who may be called upon to serve strawberries at 3 A.M., up to Captain Warwick, who has had a camp bed installed in the wheelhouse to preserve his visual acuity on stormy nights (simply travelling the lit corridor from his cabin to the wheelhouse could lose him up to 2 1/2 precious minutes before his eyes become accustomed to the darkness), the crew are attentive to the needs of all. All the while, they live a parallel existence in a part of the ship (below Deck 2) inaccessible to passengers. As well as cabins that sleep a maximum of two people, with private shower room, the crew have several bars and restaurants of their own, a library, a cinema, shops, sports hall, and a computer training room.

Magical Ports of Call

Such a range of activities and facilities might suggest that the *Queen Mary* 2 is the world's biggest holiday resort. So it is—but this resort sails the seas, crosses oceans, enters fjords, and drops anchor at the most beautiful islands. Few passengers will want to forget this. An early morning arrival in a sleepy roadstead is sure to revive the almost primitive exaltation that seizes someone woken from indolence with the cry, "Land ahoy!" Exotic ports with brilliant colours and mingling smells, their names evoke the far corners of the world: Bridgetown, Salvador de Bahia, Cartagena, Gibraltar. Some are historic ports, haunted by the memory of seamen and explorers of bygone centuries: Lisbon, Marseille, Hamburg, Southampton, Piraeus. Of the ports in the Americas, Europe, and Africa, some are large enough to accommodate the *QM2* at quayside while others are so protected that they must be approached by the even more magical means of a smaller vessel, leaving the liner at anchor in the roadstead, like the caravels of former times. And then there is New York, which lives up to everyone's expectations. To watch the forest of skyscrapers come slowly into view and the city rise up from the water; to pass the yellow Staten Island ferry on its way from Battery Park, sail past the Statue of Liberty and up the Hudson River, finally mooring at Manhattan; to follow in the footsteps of millions of Europeans who sought a new life, in the wake of the "American millionaires" who, from the beginning of the twentieth century, shuttled back and forth from the Old World to the New—all this makes for an unforgettable experience.

But mooring in small island ports is just as bewitching for those who know how to look beyond appearances—and beyond the "tourist boutiques" that line the quayside. For the arrival of a ship at an island is never a neutral event. Longed for, hoped for, and welcomed, big ships "bring wealth with them and take dreams away with them," as Jean-Rémy Villageois, a native of Martinique, so nicely puts it. Beside the *QM2*, all vessels, whether cargo ships or coasters, are mere nutshells cradled by the tropical breeze; more than any other ship, she makes the islanders dream of great cities, a mirror image of the passengers' desire for far horizons and lost paradises. One port knows this well: Fort-de-France, which extended a triumphal welcome—all dancing, bright colours, music, and flowers—to the *QM2*, its passengers, and crew, when it dropped anchor for the first time in February 2004. Captain Warwick admitted to Philip Plisson, who himself never tires of praising this "truly magical moment," that in forty years of piloting liners, he has never received a warmer welcome.

To drop anchor in an unknown land also means the opportunity to go ashore for a few hours, or to discover new countries and cities by other means: flying over St Lucia by helicopter, boarding a sporting catamaran to go observe the whales and dolphins of Dominica, diving amid the coral reefs of St Thomas, a four-wheel-drive excursion on Mt Pelée, big-game fishing at Saint-Kitts, or a visit to a sugar-cane plantation on Barbados. Whatever the choice, all must admit that the Lesser Antilles hide unsuspected treasures.

Aside from the Atlantic, which is always king, the Caribbean takes pride of place in 2005. Thirteen cruises are scheduled to visit the region, compared with just four in Europe and one in Canada. And where will the *QM2* sail in succeeding years? What untrodden route, what ports never visited by great liners, what hostile or welcoming seas will play host to her unmistakable silhouette? Her passengers will no doubt take her enough to heart to want to explore other horizons aboard her: the coasts of Africa as far as the Cape; South America; the far North; or perhaps they will accompany her in the wake of the *Laconia*, the Cunarder which in 1922 inaugurated the round-the-world cruise, an itinerary adopted to excellent effect by the *Queen Elizabeth 2*.

16/01/2002 – 22/12/2003

CONSTRUCTION

After a design phase lasting more than a year, building begins with the cutting of the first plate: a gusset or small strengthening component
all, will be assembled in the shipyard to form 3D panels weighing an average of 50 tonnes. In turn, these panels will be assembled into

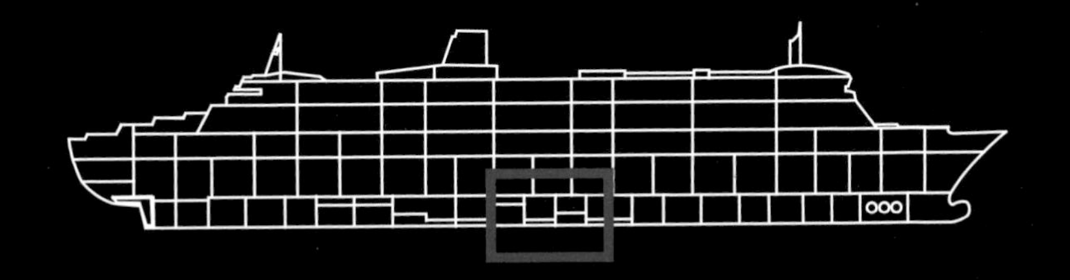

16/01/2002 – 08/2002

CUTTING OF THE FIRST PLATE AND FIRST BLOCK

weighing 10 pounds (4.5 kilograms), which will be fitted in the double hull. The cut-up sections—plates and sheets—numbering 300,000 in blocks weighing hundreds of tonnes. The finished ship will consist of about 100 blocks.

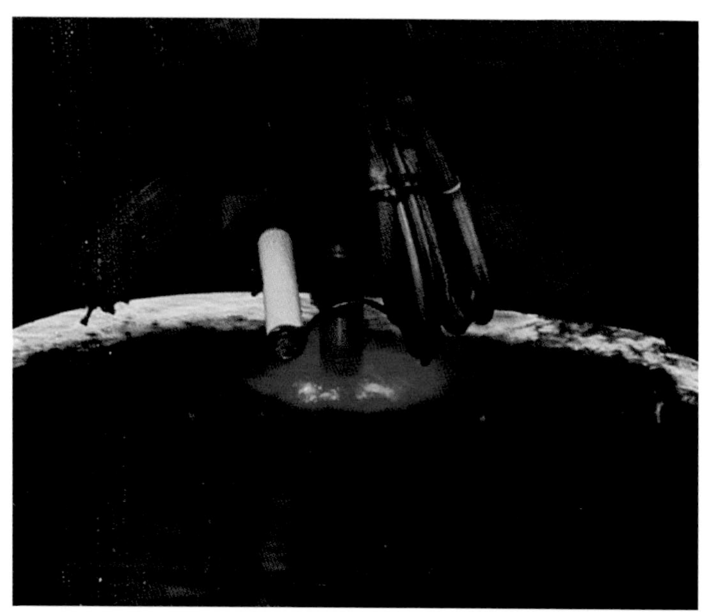

René Théveux, operating a digitally controlled machine, cuts the first plate of the *Queen Mary 2* on 16 January 2002.

Since cutting is carried out at extremely high temperatures, the plates are immersed in a bath to lessen the risk of their being warped or twisted.

ALSTOM
CHANTIERS DE L'ATLANTIQUE
ATTENTION !

Opposite, top, and middle:
Most of the hull blocks are heavily reinforced before being laid and assembled in the construction dock.

Opposite, bottom:
On 4 July 2002, the laying of Block 502, or "first block," weighing 642 tonnes, marked the beginning of the assembly phase. The ceremony, accompanied by much pomp, was attended by representatives of both the ship-owner and the shipbuilder. The date was a symbolic one: that of the first crossing by a Cunarder, the *Britannia*, on 4 July 1840.

Right:
As it does for all its ships, Chantiers de l'Atlantique gave the *QM2* a codename, "G32," when it received the order to build. This code, always consisting of a letter and two figures, is allocated by alphabetical order. The photograph shows, from top, sections of the *Queen Mary 2* (the widest block containing the engines); the *Crystal Serenity* (H32); the *MSC Lirica* (K32); and finally of the *Island Princess* (D32). Among them, these ships fill the entire construction dock at Chantiers de l'Atlantique, which is more than half a mile (1 kilometre) long. Just a few months after starting work on the *QM2*, Chantiers de l'Atlantique had already run through much of the alphabet; codename R32 (eleven ships down the line from G32) was allocated in July 2004.

P 40

Right and following double-page spread:
10 August 2002 saw the first transfer to the construction dock. This was the first time the *Queen Mary 2* moved from her berth.

P 42

CHANTIERS DE L'
TIQUE

Assembly of the hull gathers pace in September 2002. The "cathedrals" of Saint-Nazaire—gigantic gantries visible from a great distance and form the ship's hull, which will take four months to assemble in its entirety. By then, the ship will weigh 27,830 tonnes.

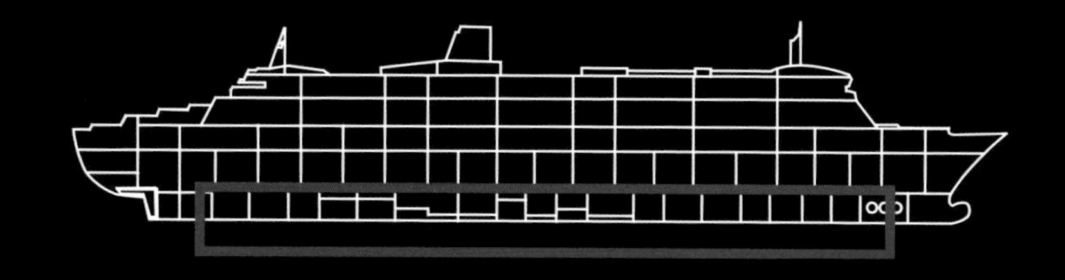

09/2002 - 12/2002

ASSEMBLY OF THE BASE AND SECOND

operated by just one man—perform their dance. Once out of the construction workshops, the huge steel blocks are placed on the stocks to

MOVEMENT

Above, and following double-page spread:
On 27 August 2002, four enormous diesel engines are installed. Each produces 16 megawatts; two 25-megawatt turbines will complete the *Queen Mary 2*'s power generation plant.

Layher

CHANTIERS DE L'ATLANTIQUE

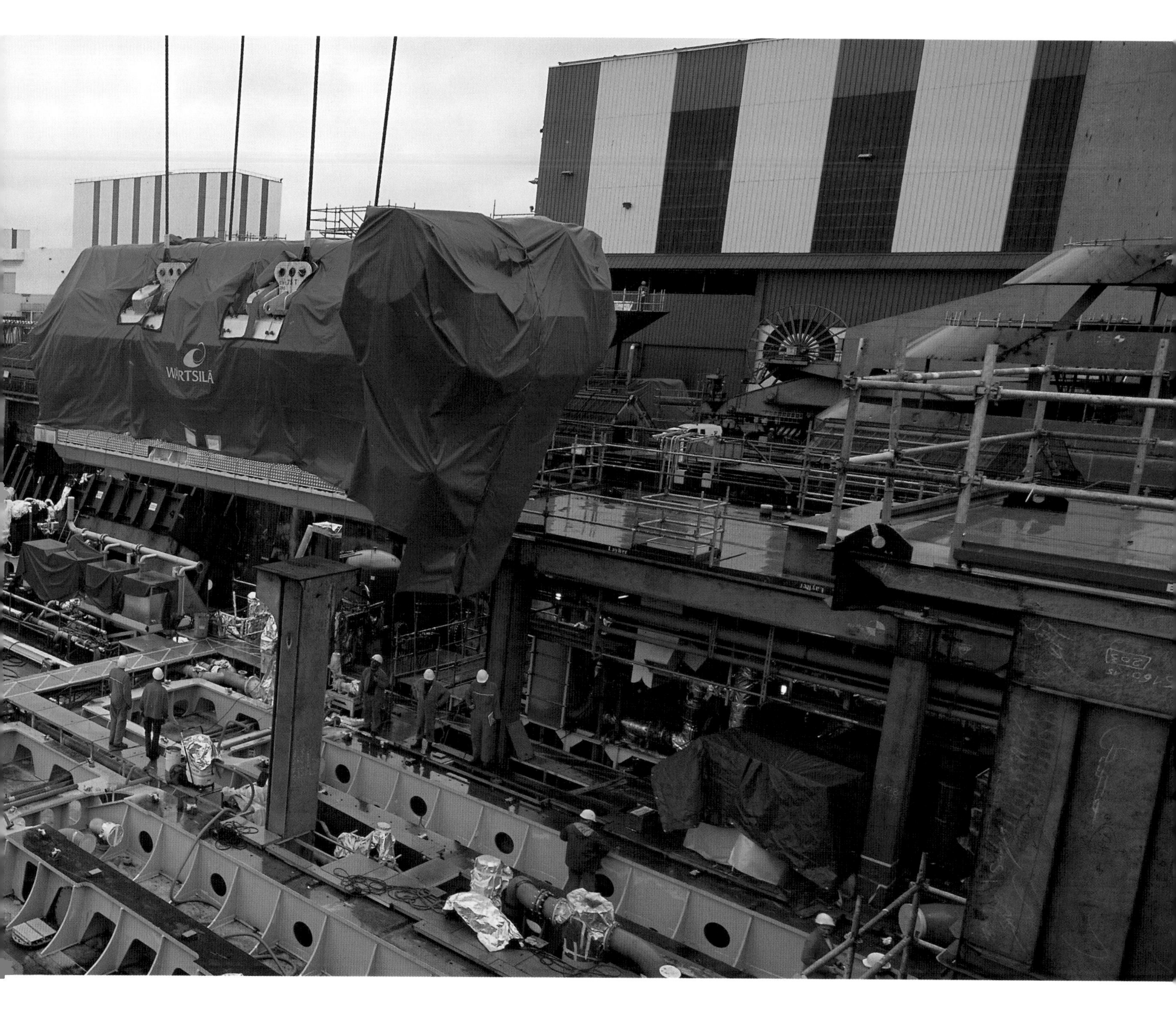
WÄRTSILÄ

Left:
The slings are prepared before the blocks are lifted.

Right:
A forest of scaffolding springs up round the ship as her hull takes shape.

ENTREPOSE
ENTREPOSE
ENTREPOSE
ENTREPOSE
ENTREPOSE
ENTREPOSE

The loggias of decks 4, 5, and 6 take shape. Only the lower decks have windows, while the upper decks have balconies.

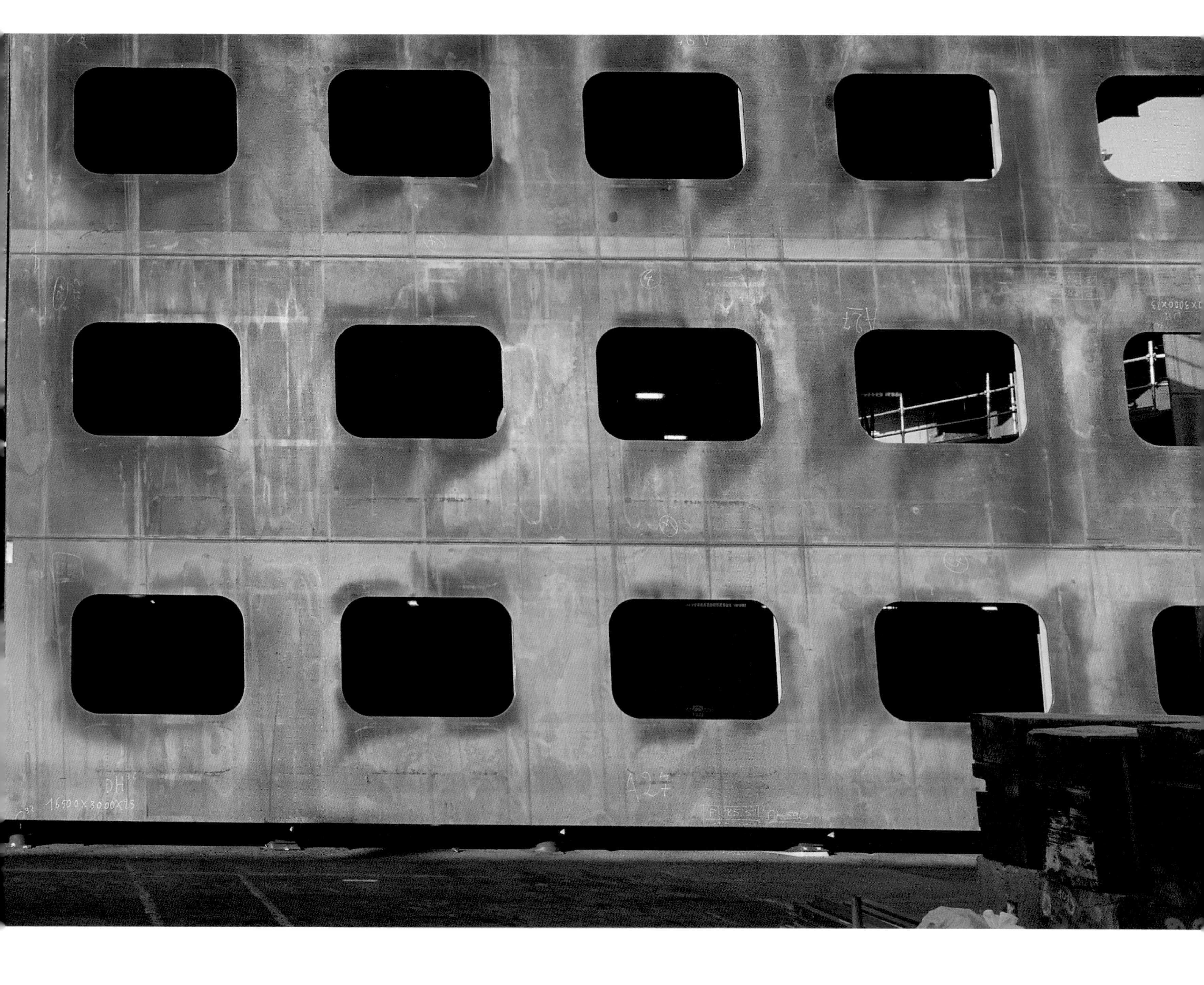

Cross-section of the stern. A view of the keel, double hull, the hull's sides, and the first blocks of the superstructure.

Left:
Interior of a block. Care and concentration during work allow for meticulous checking.

Below:
A lengthwise view conveys the scale of the shipyard.

P 58

1 December 2002. Five months after it was placed on the stocks, the ship is almost ready to glide to the deep dock for completion of the metal hull. In the foreground, the hole in the forward part of the *QM2* shows where the auditorium will be located, giving an idea of the structure's extreme complexity.

P 59

Last-minute preparations are under way before the transfer to the deep section of the dock. The *QM2* must be moved forward a few tens of metres to make room for another ship to be built. It will take eight hours to fill the 885-metre construction dock with water.

2 Dock B :
1 December 2002 to 21 March 2003. By the end of this phase, the *QM2* will weigh almost 50,000 tonnes.

1 Dock A :
4 July 2002 to 30 November 2002. At the end of this stage, the *QM2* approaches 28,000 tonnes in weight.

Right:
The *QM2* is now in deep dock, closer to the Loire estuary. At this stage she weighs exactly 27,830 tonnes and is made up of 45 blocs. By the time she is complete, these will number about 100.

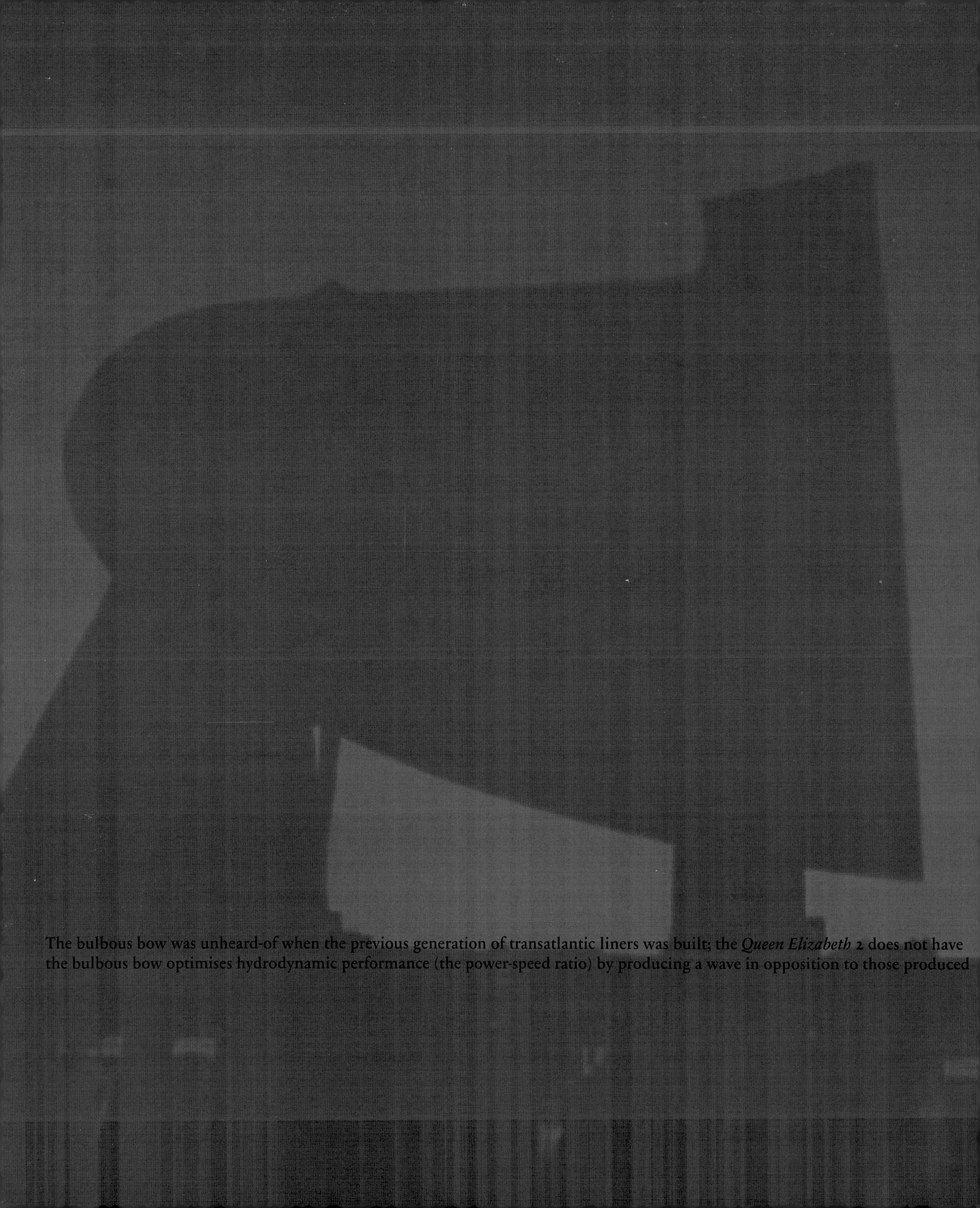

The bulbous bow was unheard-of when the previous generation of transatlantic liners was built; the *Queen Elizabeth* 2 does not have
the bulbous bow optimises hydrodynamic performance (the power-speed ratio) by producing a wave in opposition to those produced

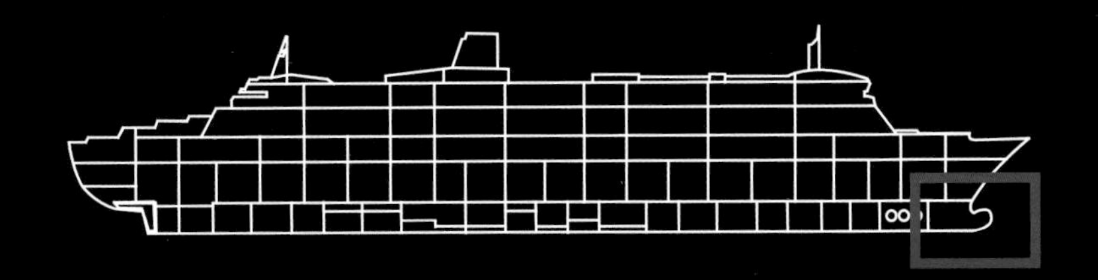

10/2002 - 12/2002

INSTALLATION OF THE

one. Today, however, it is fitted to all large vessels. A hollow attachment three decks high, welded to the front of the hull at the waterline, by the ship's forward movement through the water, which would otherwise slow her down.

BULBOUS BOW

Above:
Slings are used to unload the bulbous bow on its arrival from the shipyards of Gdansk, Poland, where it was built.

Right:
Cross-section of the forward part of the ship before fitting of the bulbous bow. In the foreground are the three thrusters, with a combined power of 3 megawatts. Above these, the cabin decks have already been fitted with pipework and ventilation ducts. Seen from outside, the hull is taking shape; within, fitting-out is in full swing.

14 December 2002, 7 A.M.
The bulbous bow has been welded to the hull. Plate workers are putting the finishing touches.

The bulbous bow has been assembled, and the lower part of the stem laid. The hull is now complete.

The elegant rounded stern of the *Queen Mary 2* is typical of the great transatlantic liners of the last century, and is also very effective in
improves hydrodynamic performance. The result is a hybrid stern, designed by Cunard's naval architect especially for the *QM2*.

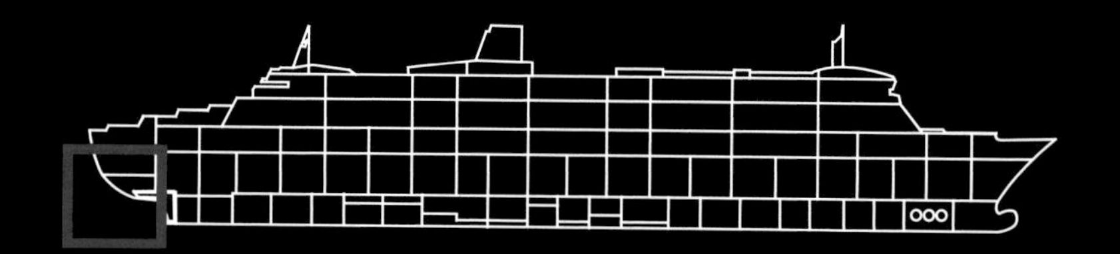

16/01/2003

REAR QUARTER-DECK

reducing pitching in rough weather. Beneath the waterline, meanwhile, the lower part of the hull has a tauter, more vertical outline, which

LOWER PART OF THE HULL

Opposite, above, and following pages:
These "pyramids" have been specially designed to support the immense weight of the rear of the ship before it is welded to the rest of the hull. They will be used only once.

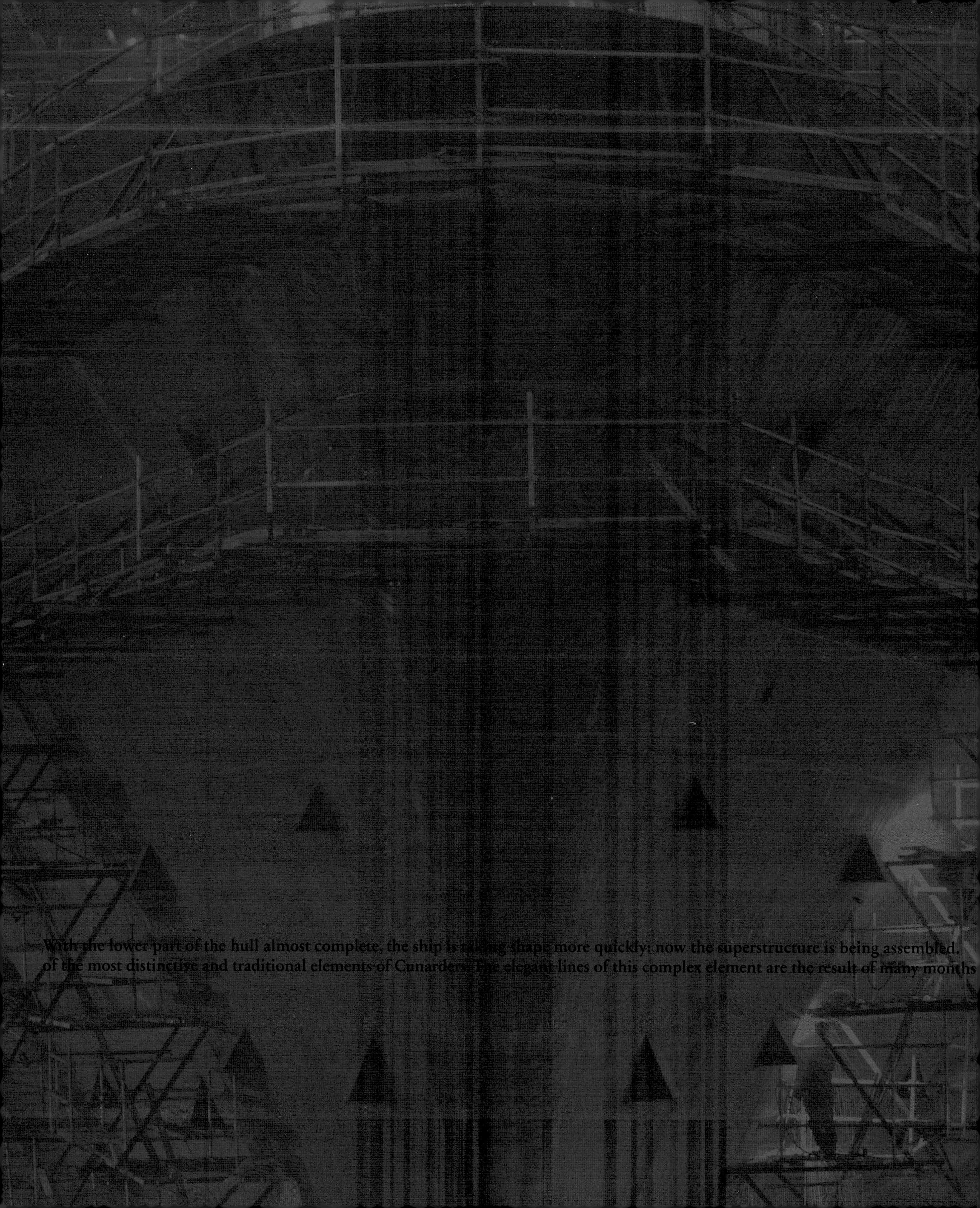

With the lower part of the hull almost complete, the ship is taking shape more quickly: now the superstructure is being assembled.
of the most distinctive and traditional elements of Cunarders. The elegant lines of this complex element are the result of many months

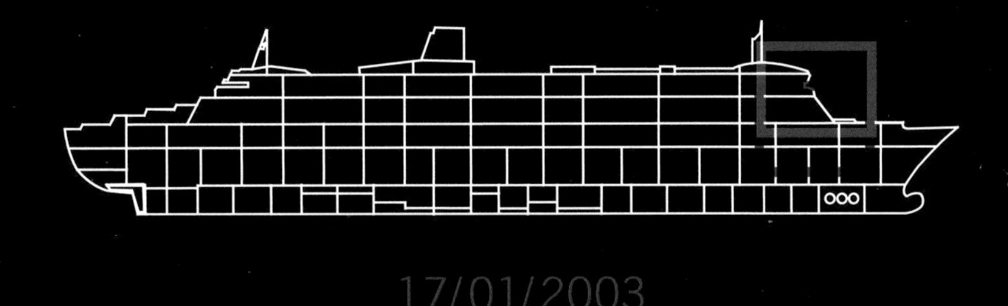

17/01/2003

INSTALLATION OF

Together with the funnel, the curved façade of the superstructure of the *Queen Mary 2*, which echoes that of the first *Queen Mary*, is one of work in the engineering and design department. It will take only a few hours to lay the 627-tonne block.

THE FAÇADE

P 82

17 January 2003. In Saint-Nazaire's early-morning mist, the façade (627 tonnes) looks like a UFO.

Opposite:
A few minutes before it is laid, the superstructure façade hangs from the gantry.

Following double-page spread:
The first two "passengers" inaugurate the observation deck, which will offer the same view as the captain has from the bridge.

The stem, built to withstand the North Atlantic.

Top:
Fitting-out work in the observation lounge.

Left:
Blocks are welded together.

The façade is slowly lowered above the stem by the large gantry's two main hoists.

At intervals of a few days, between 27 January and 4 February 2003, the three blocks that most embody the identity of the *Queen Mary 2*
to cut softly through the great swell of the North Atlantic, which is often violent in winter. This slim, keen bow will sport the ship's

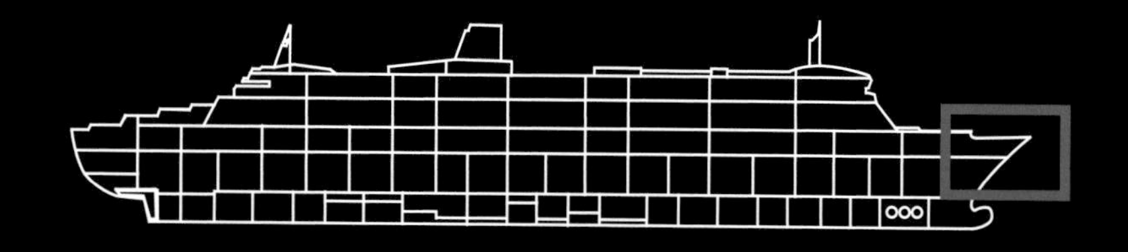

27/01/2003

INSTALLATION OF THE STEM

are laid: the stem, the upper part of the stern, and the wheelhouse. Weighing 381 tonnes, the stem is a magnificent, streamlined V, ready
name and give the vessel her proud bearing.

LSTOM

27 January 2003. The liner's stem against the Saint-Nazaire sky.

A few minutes before lifting, the fabricators and sling operators fix the slings to the 381-tonne block using special chains.

The stem marries up with the curve of the hull. The liner is starting to take shape.

The quarter deck—the last block of the stern, weighing 424 tonnes—is rounded as in all transatlantic liners, and bears the vessel's their appearance. The traditional stern swimming pools will be installed on them.

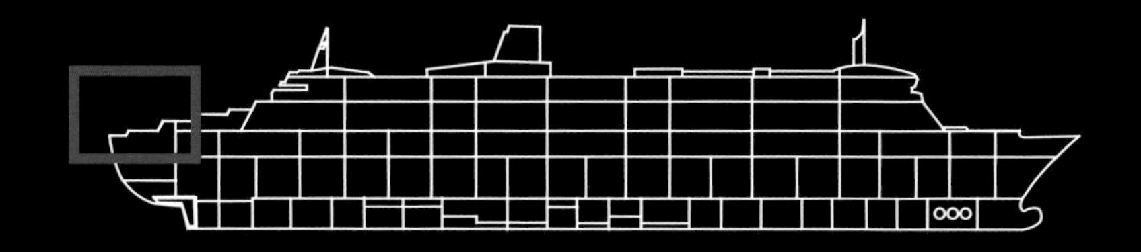

01/02/2003

REAR QUARTER-DECK

name and that of her home port, Southampton. With this block, the famous tiered stern decks typical of transatlantic liners make

UPPER SECTION

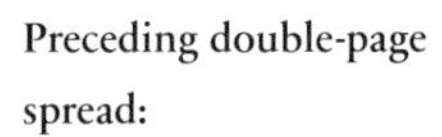

Preceding double-page spread:
In the foreground, the *QM2* takes up the whole of Dock B. Just behind, the preassembly area can be glimpsed, as well as the panel fabrication workshops. In the distance, the "180 tonnes" yard; and beyond, the town of Saint-Nazaire.

Right:
Seen from below, the taut lines of the hull contrast with the afterpeak.

The swimming pools and Jacuzzis are installed on decks 6, 7, and 8. The open decks of the stern were fitted out well before the block was laid in the construction dock.

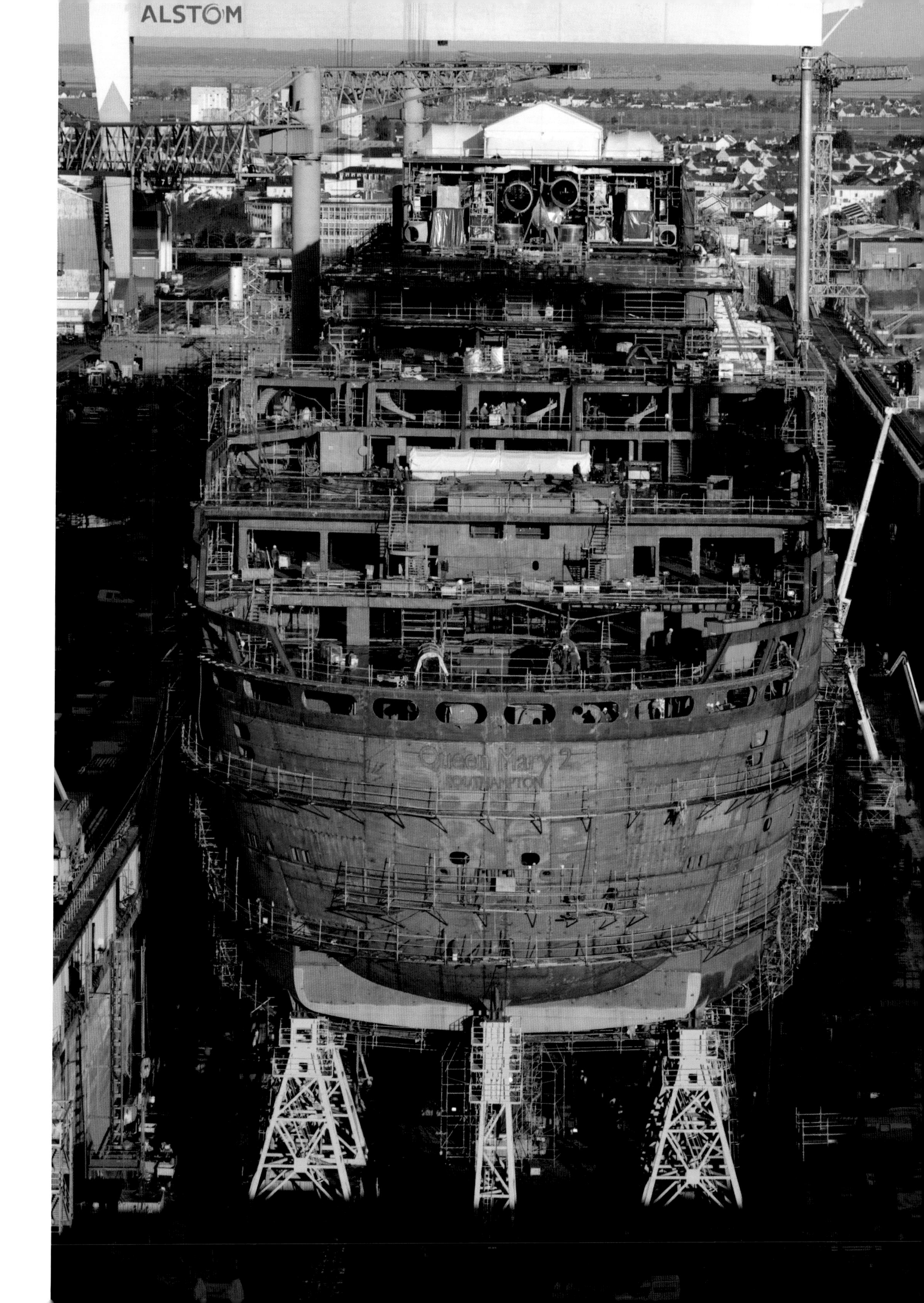
ALSTOM
Queen Mary 2
SOUTHAMPTON

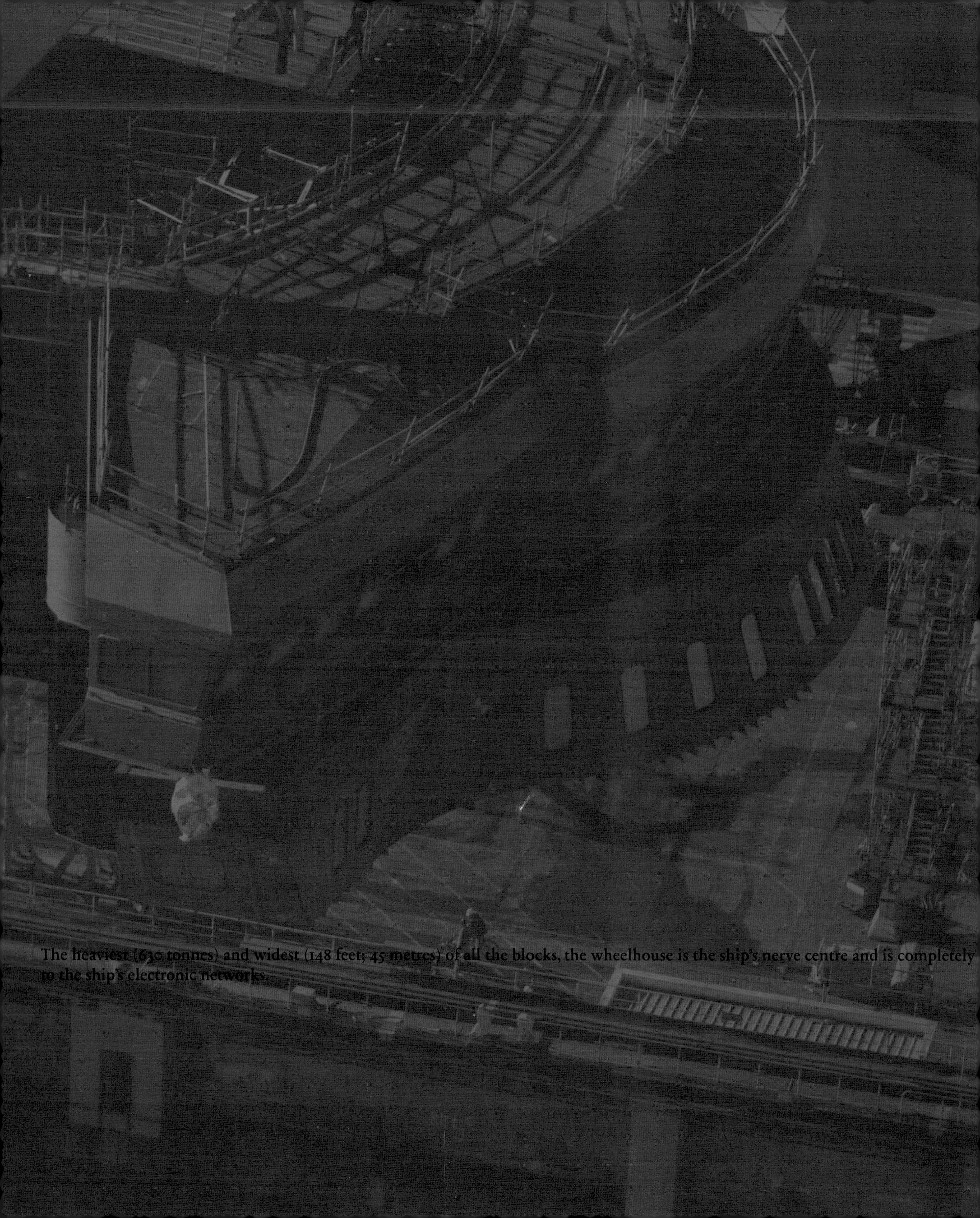

The heaviest (630 tonnes) and widest (148 feet; 45 metres) of all the blocks, the wheelhouse is the ship's nerve centre and is completely
to the ship's electronic networks.

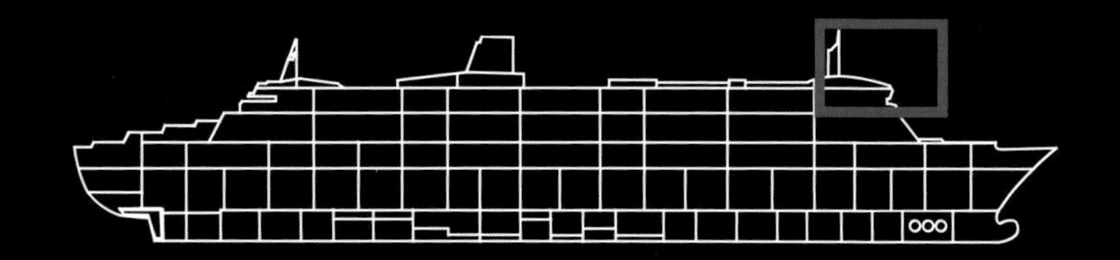

04/02/2003

INSTALLATION OF

fitted out before even being laid in place. Command consoles, computers, and control screens are all fitted. Later, they will be connected

THE WHEELHOUSE

ALSTOM

Preceding double-page spread:
4 February 2003. The large gantry of Chantiers de l'Atlantique (750 tonnes of lifting capacity) faces the *QM2*, ready to lay the wheelhouse.

Right:
Because of its size and complex shape (it stretches over several decks) the wheelhouse is the trickiest block to lay in place. It will be lowered with micrometric precision.

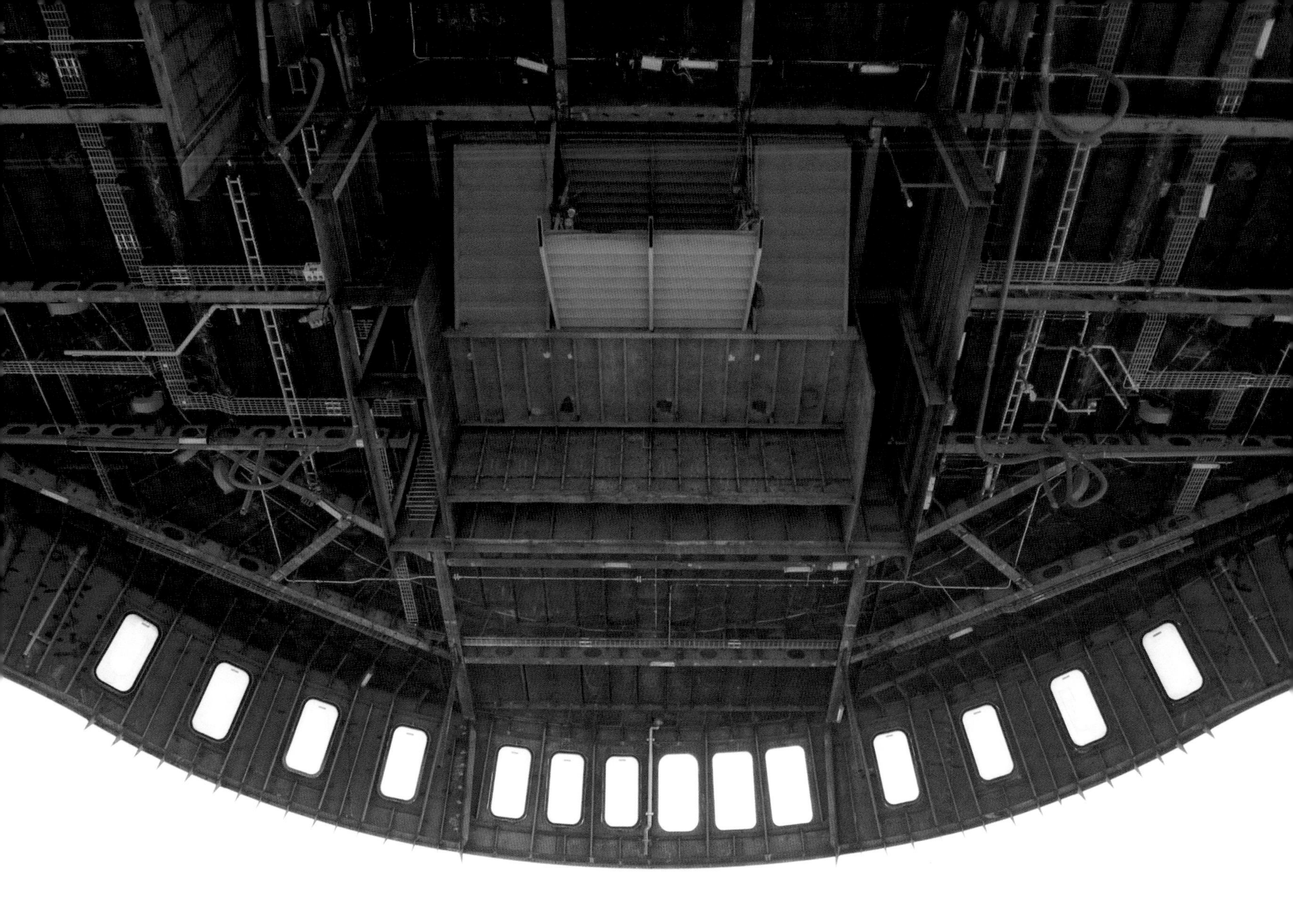

Left:
A few minutes before the laying operation, the final adjustments are made.

Above:
Block 850 silhouetted against the sky. In the centre is one of the staircases that will lead to Deck 10.

The workers will move back a step to allow the crane operator to lay the block.

The ship rests on a line of stocks (blocks made of wood and concrete). They are lined up using a system of lasers to make them able to bear the 50,000-tonne hull without deforming it in any way.

With its red-and-black bands, emblematic of Cunard, the funnel of the *QM2* was built in its entirety at the heart of Chantiers de l'Atlantique.
lermakers and engineers. The first element of the funnel was laid in March 2003, but the "cap" was not put in place until 4 April, in the fitting-

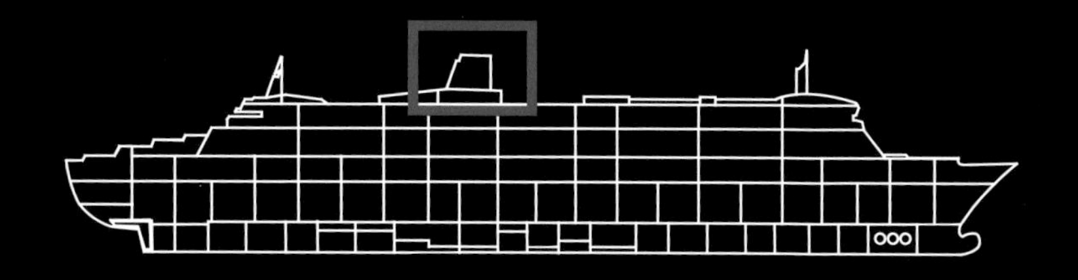

03/2003 – 04/2003

INSTALLATION OF THE FUNNEL

A single piece of metal almost 40 feet (12 metres) high, shaped by hand in a single operation so that no weld is discernible, it is the pride of the out dock, because it brought the liner up to her full height of 236 feet (72 metres) and could not have passed under the gantries in the assembly dock.

Above:
13 March 2003: the 145-tonne funnel, the black-and-red emblem of Cunard, is hoisted on board the liner.

Opposite:
Waste-ducts from turbines, diesel engines, and kitchens: the interior of the funnel has been used to the utmost, and not a square metre remains unoccupied.

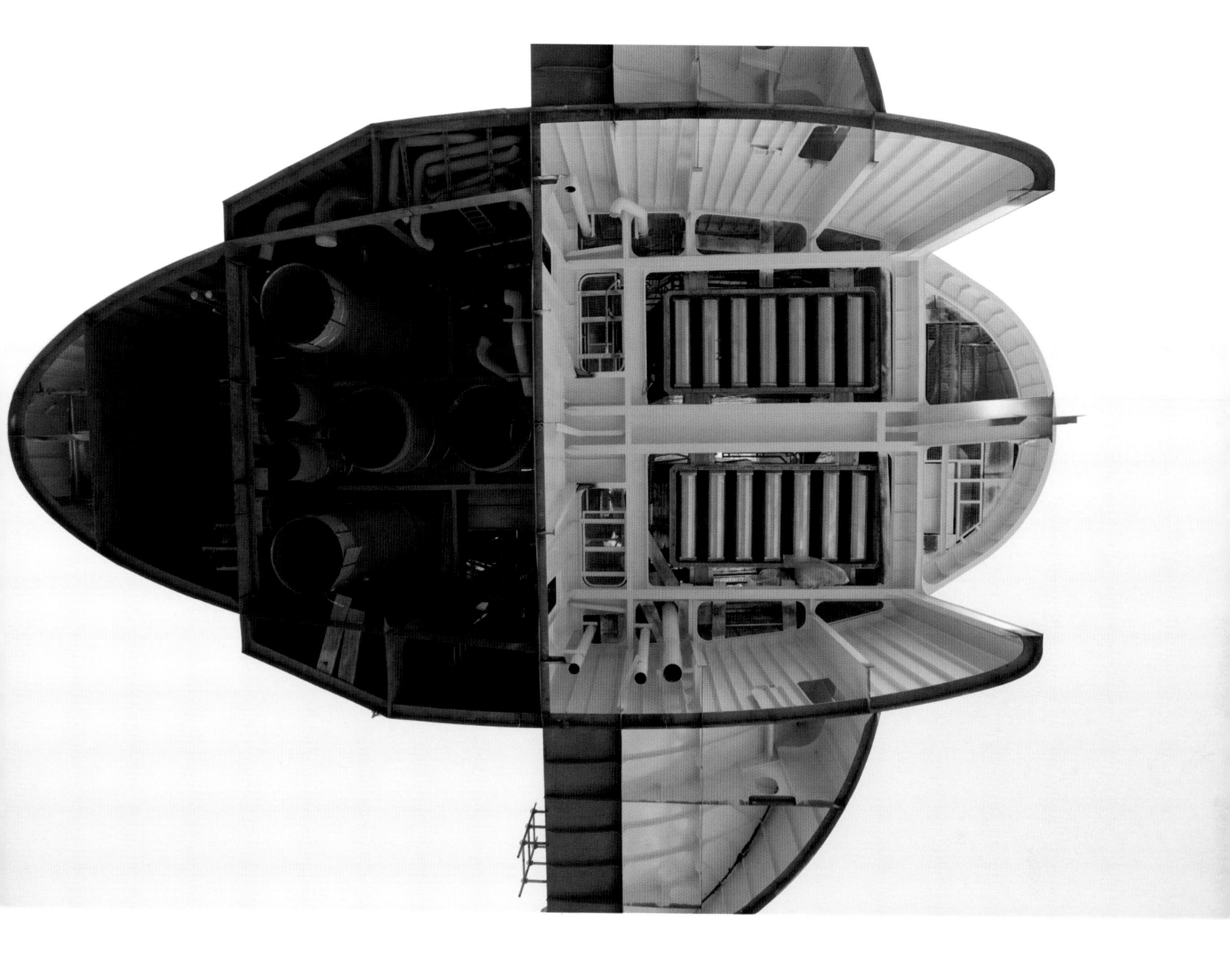

The hull is complete: now for the fitting-out. A landmark is passed when the ship takes to the water to be transferred about a quarter-
the 1970s. There, the *QM2* will be fitted out like a veritable floating town. This is the first moment of truth for the Chantiers de

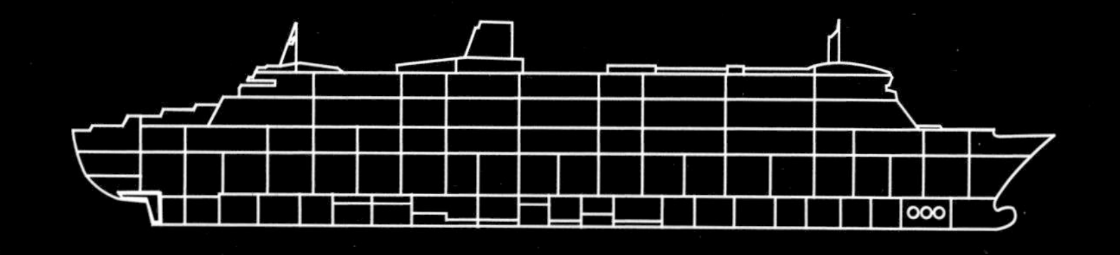

21/03/2003

TRANSFER TO THE FITTING-OUT DOCK

mile from the building dock (Dock B) to the fitting-out dock (Dock C, a few hundred metres downstream), which had not been dry since l'Atlantique, and a great moment for the crowd that has thronged to the harbour's entry at 5 A.M.

Final preparations for the transfer. The ship now weighs 50,000 tonnes.

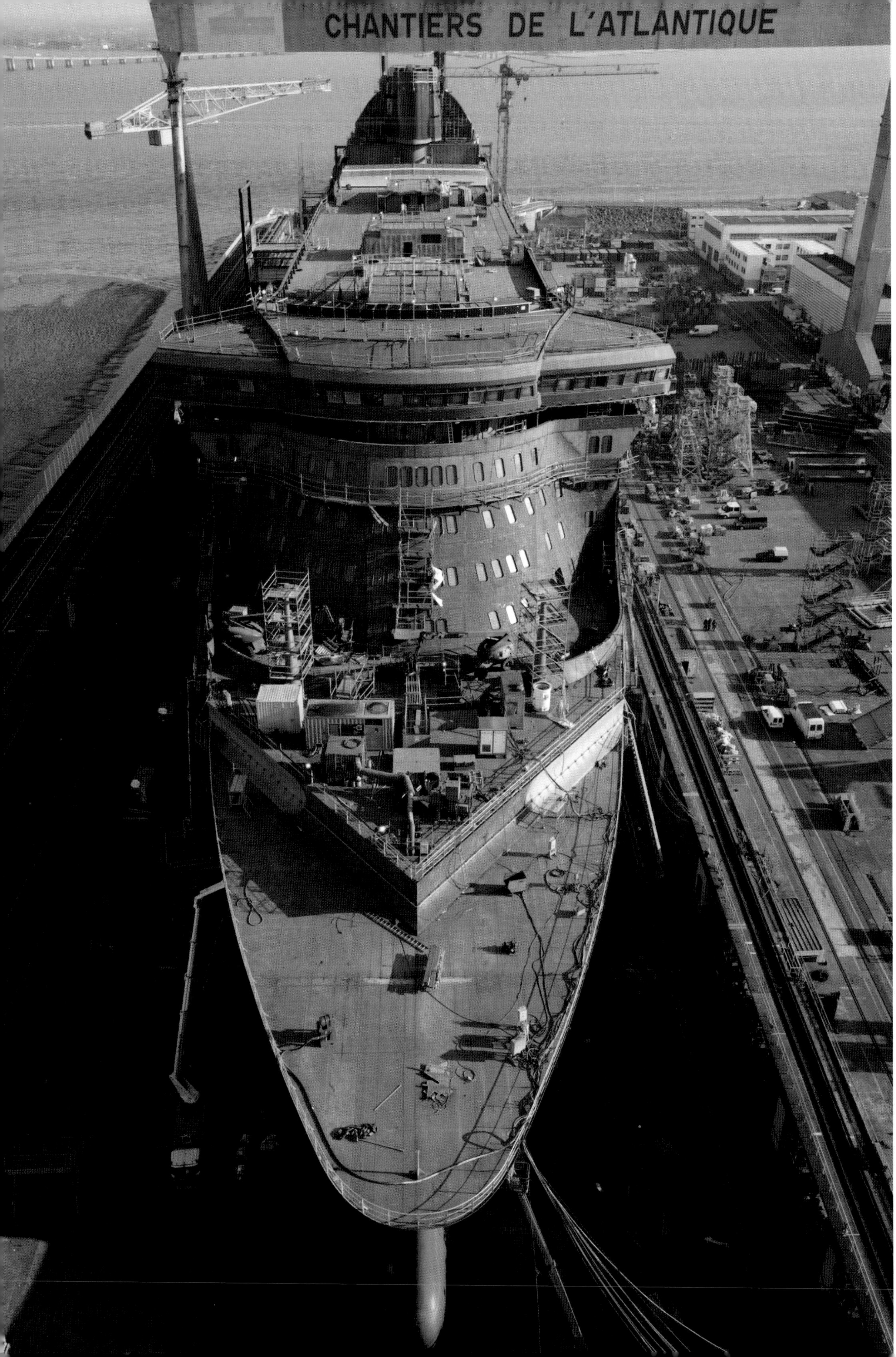
CHANTIERS DE L'ATLANTIQUE

P 128

Modern, flat-bottomed construction docks have replaced the sloping ones formerly used. Thus, the *QM2* will not be launched in the same way as the *France* and the *Normandie*.

16 March 2003. The radar mast is put in place, and the traditional Carnival mast-stepping ceremony is transformed into a great event, the "dry-dock party." Here, 300 guests pose for Philip Plisson.

Preceding double-page spread:
19 March 2003. A few hours before the ship takes to the water for the transfer, the deep dock has been evacuated completely.

Below:
20 March 2003. Assembly of the hull has taken just eight months. The deep dock is now flooded once more, and the *QM2* is ready to enter the Loire estuary on her way to the fitting-out dock.

21 March 2003, 5 A.M. The *QM2*'s first "cruise." Escorted by eight tugs, the liner glides the quarter mile or so (a few hundred metres) along the Loire to reach the fitting-out dock.

The queen takes up her quarters in the fitting-out dock, 1,390 feet long and 311 wide (424 metres by 95), still known as "Dock C." Designed for building million-tonne supertankers, the dock had not been dry since the 1970s. Fitting-out is a vast operation that requires immense pieces of equipment.

In the foreground, the three stem thrusters are hidden behind heavy doors. These will remain closed for normal navigation to allow optimum water flow round the hull, and will only be opened for manoeuvres in harbour. Higher up, on decks 7 to 12, plastic covers protect painting operations on the balconies from the weather. Between decks 7 and 8 are the davits: these await the lifeboats, which will only be put in place at the last moment, just before setting sail.

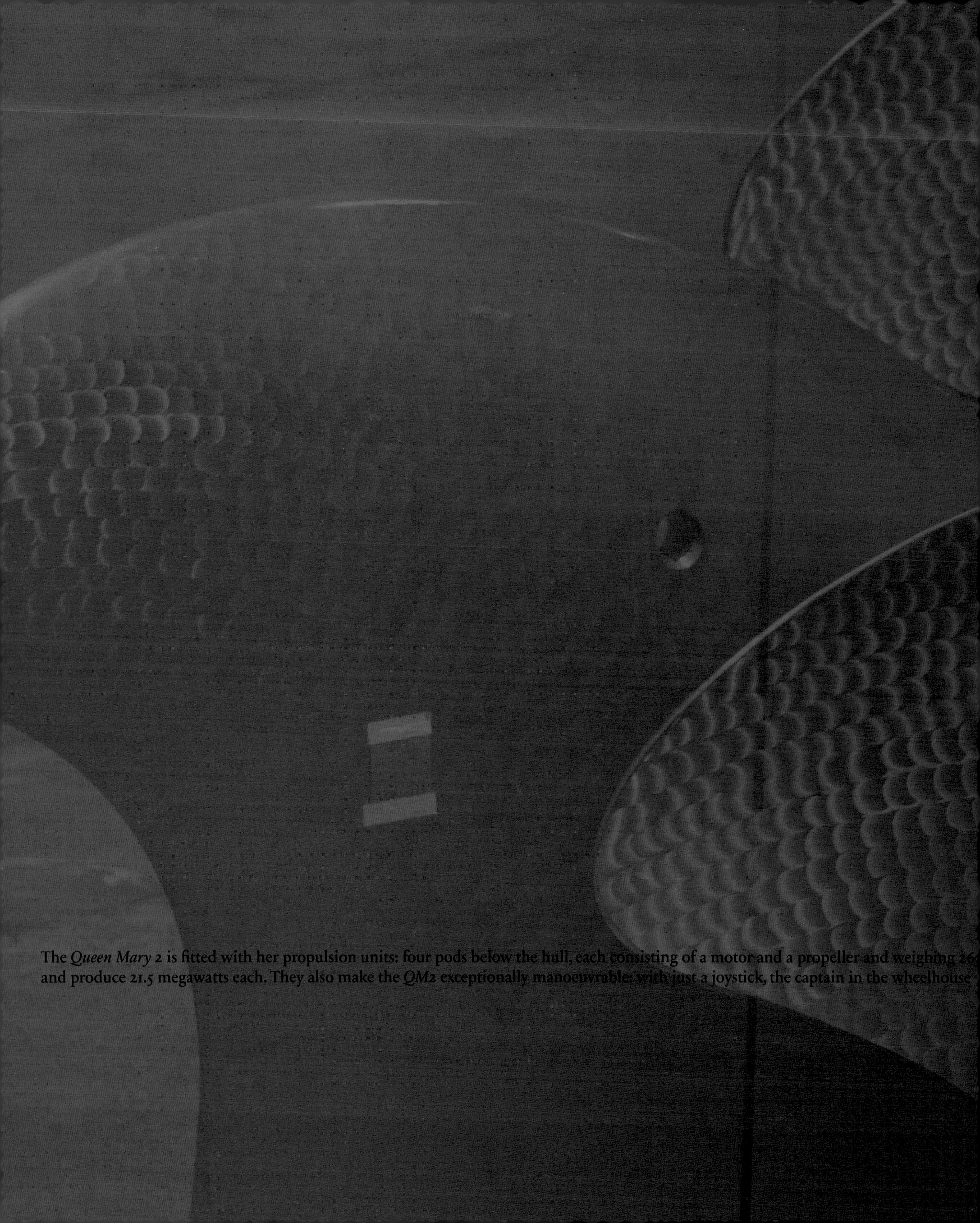

The *Queen Mary 2* is fitted with her propulsion units: four pods below the hull, each consisting of a motor and a propeller and weighing 26
and produce 21.5 megawatts each. They also make the *QM2* exceptionally manoeuvrable: with just a joystick, the captain in the wheelhouse

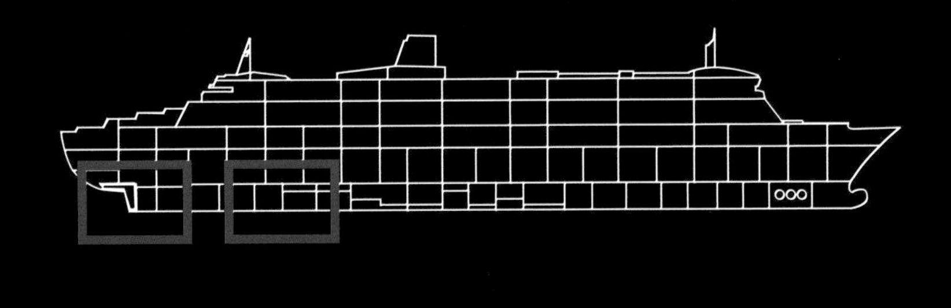

07/2003

ASSEMBLY OF THE PROPELLERS AND PODS

tonnes apiece. Two are fixed, and two can swivel over 360 degrees. The *QM2*'s Rolls Royce pods are the biggest and most powerful ever built, controls the four pods and three stem thrusters to manoeuvre the ship in port.

Left:
The stainless steel propeller blades have been specially designed to drive the ship at speeds of almost 30 knots, while keeping to a minimum noise and vibrations transmitted to the hull and the passengers.

Opposite:
The pods are brought underneath the hull before being hoisted in position by a system of jacks.

Below:
The ship is fitted with four pods weighing 260 tonnes each. The two fixed pods are forward; the two azimuthal ones are at the stern, and will be used to manoeuvre the ship.

Following double-page spread:
The propulsion system is now in place. The first sea trials are a mere two months away. July and August will be spent on commissioning the propulsion system. The countdown begins for the teams of mechanics and engineers.

3
2
LOXAM
ACCESS
02 40 66 09 01
LOXAM
ACCESS

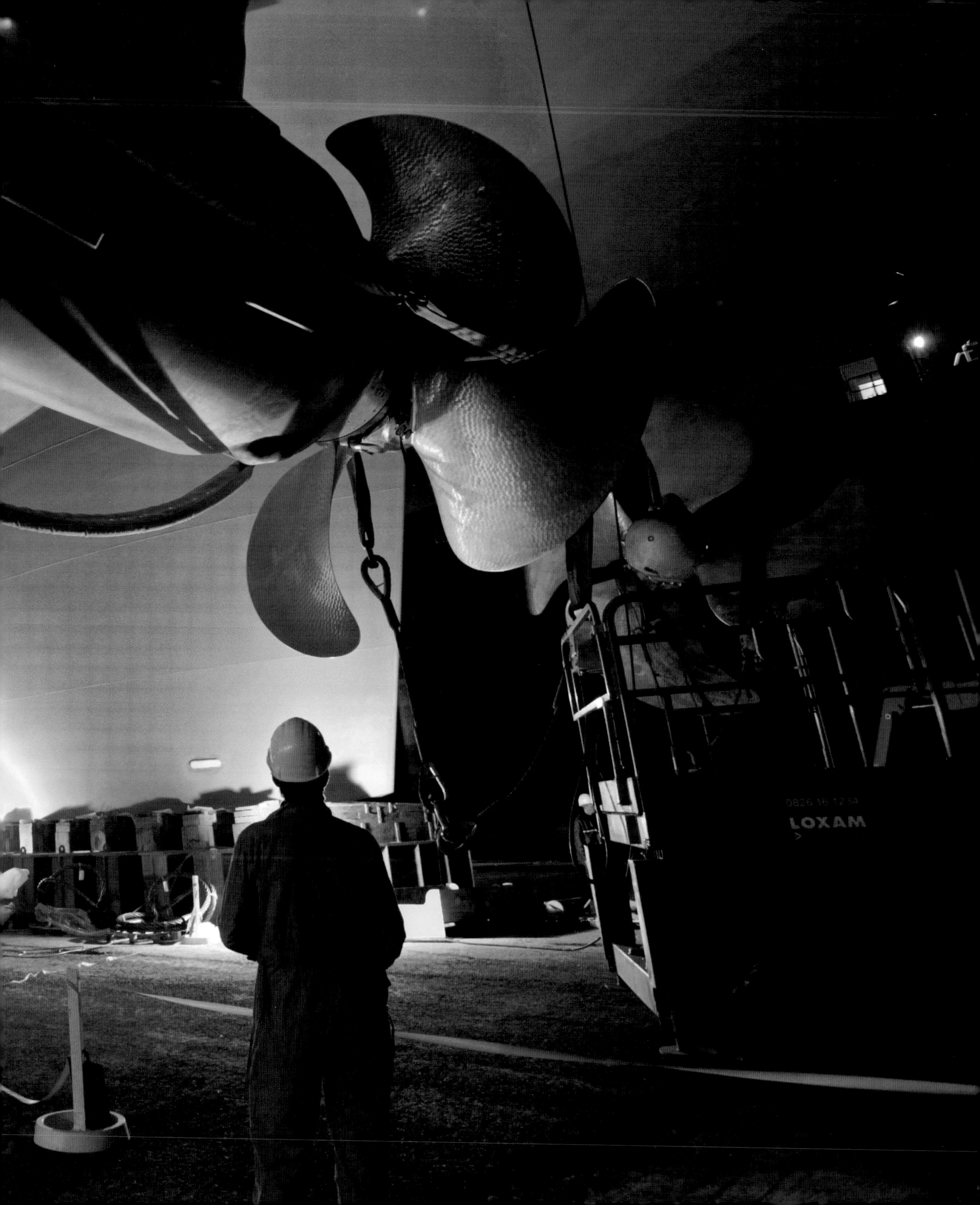
LOXAM

September and November 2003: two series of trials will be enough for the engineers and technicians of Chantiers de l'Atlantique to check the
with the ship-owner. A multitude of admirers comes to witness the *QM2*'s first outing: 40,000 people on land and at sea—compared with just 45

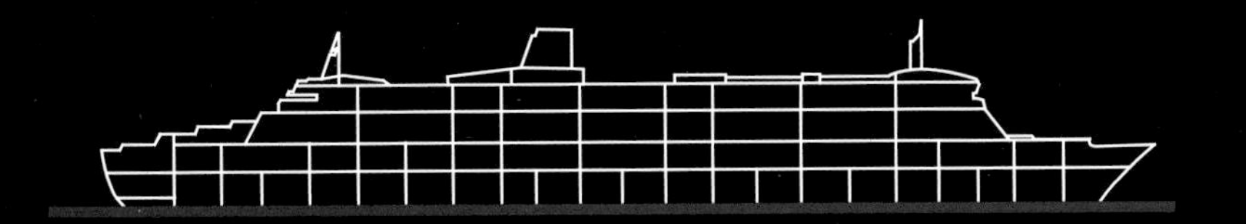

25-29/09/2003 – 7-11/11/2003

SEA

power generation, propulsion, navigation system, radars, and anchor-lowering system, and to confirm that they perform as stipulated in the contract on board: engineers, technicians, and representatives of the ship-owner, who spend four days sailing back and forth between Belle-Île and L'île d'Yeu.

TRIALS

Above:
Thursday 25 September 2003, 5:09 P.M. the ship is ready for her first sea trials. The curious throng the shipyard's perimeter; farther along the coast, a huge crowd awaits the passage of the giant of the seas.

Opposite:
5:12 P.M.: the *QM2*'s first manoeuvre on the Loire, helped by tugs from Saint-Nazaire.

Above and following double-page spread: Thousands of pairs of eyes, five tugs, and tens of craft accompany the first journey of the *QM2* towards the open sea. A large escort accompanies her along the coast as far as Saint-Marc, where she heads out to sea for her first trials.

CUNARD

Queen Mary 2

Bird's-eye view of the bulbous bow. The trim and flotation of the ship have been adjusted to an optimal level: the bulbous bow just breaks the surface for the first sea trials. On this trip the ship will reach a maximum of 29.21 knots, which she will exceed on her second outing with a speed of 29.62 knots.

Pod control. More than 100 sensors were specially installed within the pods for the trials. Teams worked in shifts, permanently monitoring their working parameters.

Machine command post. The engineers control increases in speed, and the power generator and propulsion system are under close surveillance.

In the wheelhouse, a few minutes before the speed trials begin. The ship's performance is confirmed for Jean-Rémy Villageois, *QM2* project manager (in the foreground, at the chart table, checking the provisional speed run trajectory), and commander Selosse (in the background), who commanded the *QM2* on her sea trials.

Manoeuvrability trials confirm the predictions of hydrodynamic engineers:
– Ship travelling at 26.6 knots
– Helm angle: 28 degrees
– Start of turning circle (shown in the photographs)

The ship barely lists and responds perfectly to the controls. Measurements of noise and vibrations give further confirmation of the vessel's excellent performance.

Even when the propulsion system is pushed to the maximum (86 megawatts), almost no vibration is felt on board.

Anchor trials. The ship is stationary, ready to drop anchor, and the anchor emerges from its hawsehole.

P 162

At low speed, the bulbous bow appears to be embraced by the wave produced by the stem.

Following double-page spread:
The light shows up the ship's still-unfinished state. Painting will resume as soon as the *QM2* returns to the shipyard.

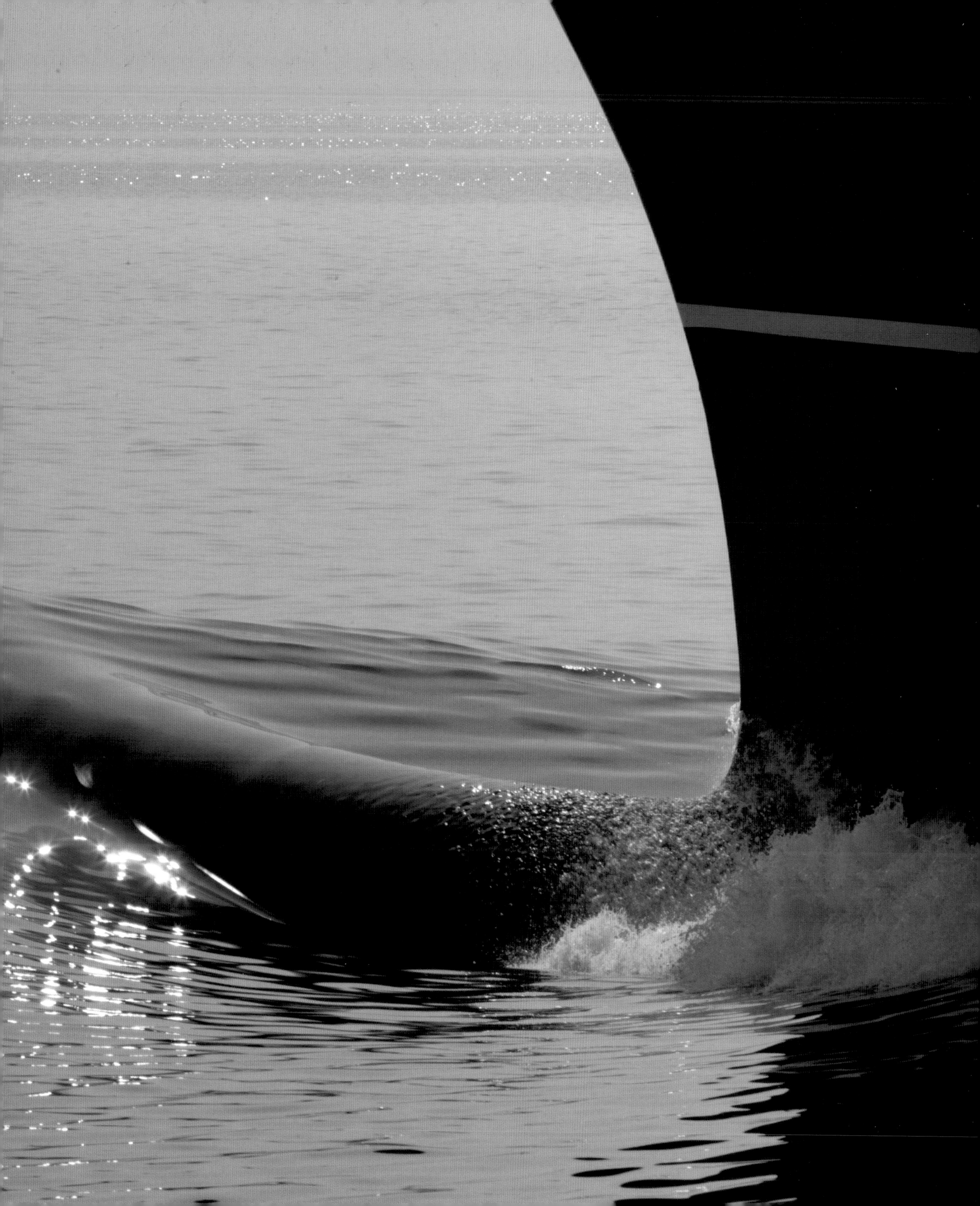

CUNARD

CUNARD

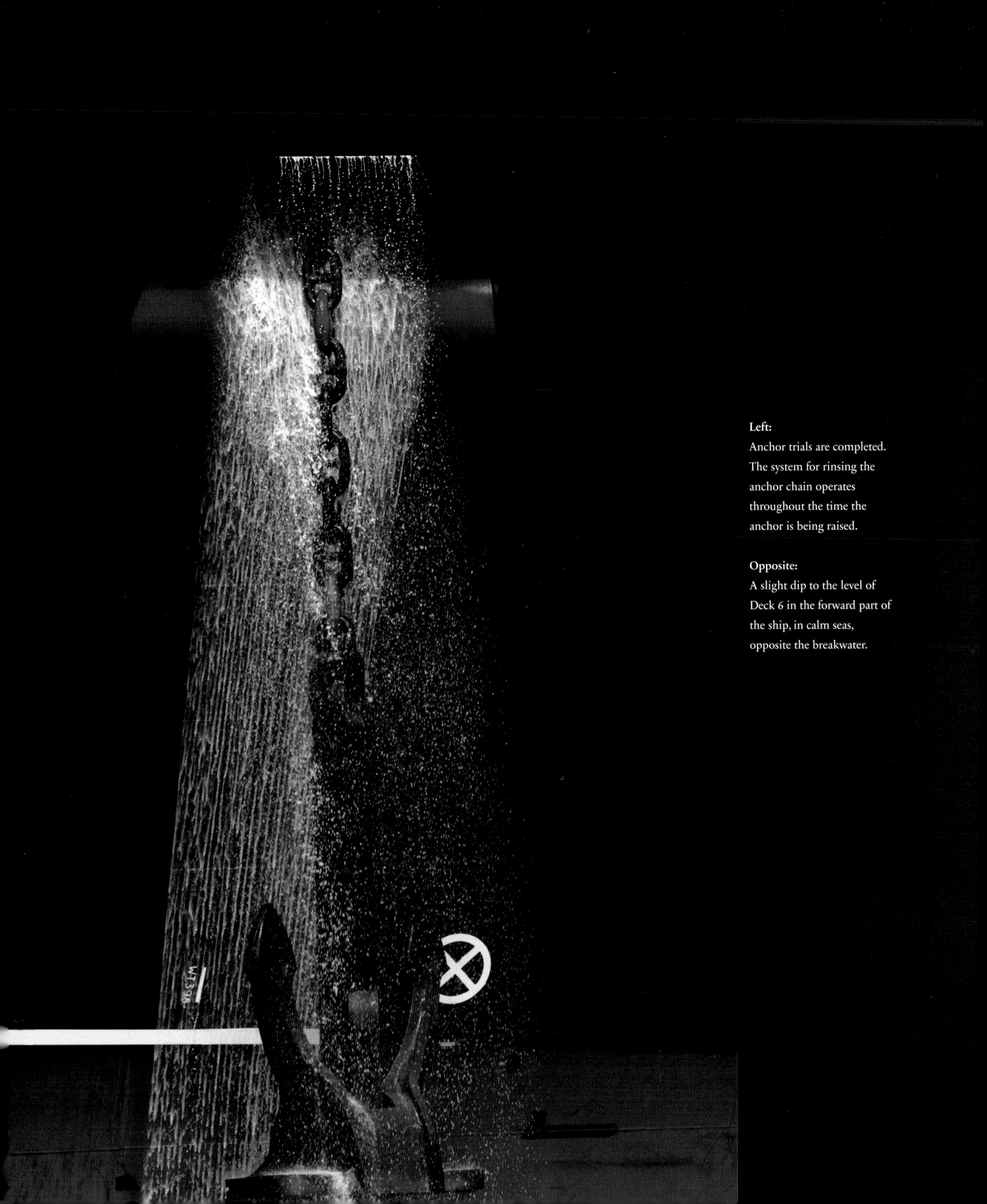

Left:
Anchor trials are completed. The system for rinsing the anchor chain operates throughout the time the anchor is being raised.

Opposite:
A slight dip to the level of Deck 6 in the forward part of the ship, in calm seas, opposite the breakwater.

29 September 2003. The first sea trials have proved conclusive. The ship returns to her tugs before beginning the manoeuvre of reentry to the shipyard. A small customs vessel, the Épée, has escorted the giant throughout this phase, except during the speed trials, when the *QM2* left her far behind several times.

Queen Mary 2

Queen Mary 2

With her colours applied, the *Queen Mary 2* attains her full brilliance. A total of 400 tonnes of paint were needed to cover the nearly 6
be the flagship: Federal Grey for the hull, red beneath the waterline, Cunard Orange for the funnel, and white for the superstructure.

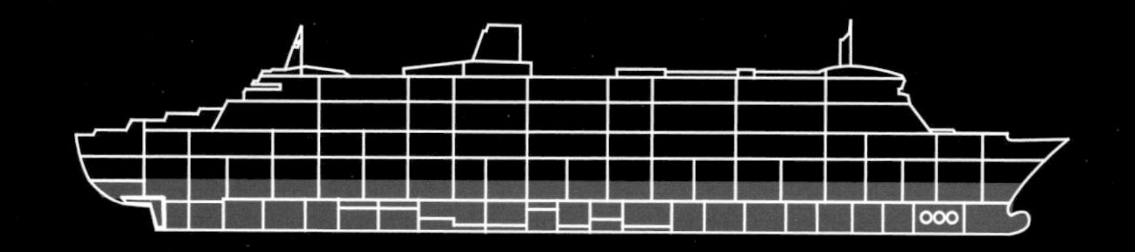

10/2003

COLOURS

million square feet (550,000 square metres) of the *QM2* with the traditional colours of the Cunard fleet, of which she will henceforth
Regulatory markings, precise and discreet, have been painted carefully by hand.

AND MARKINGS

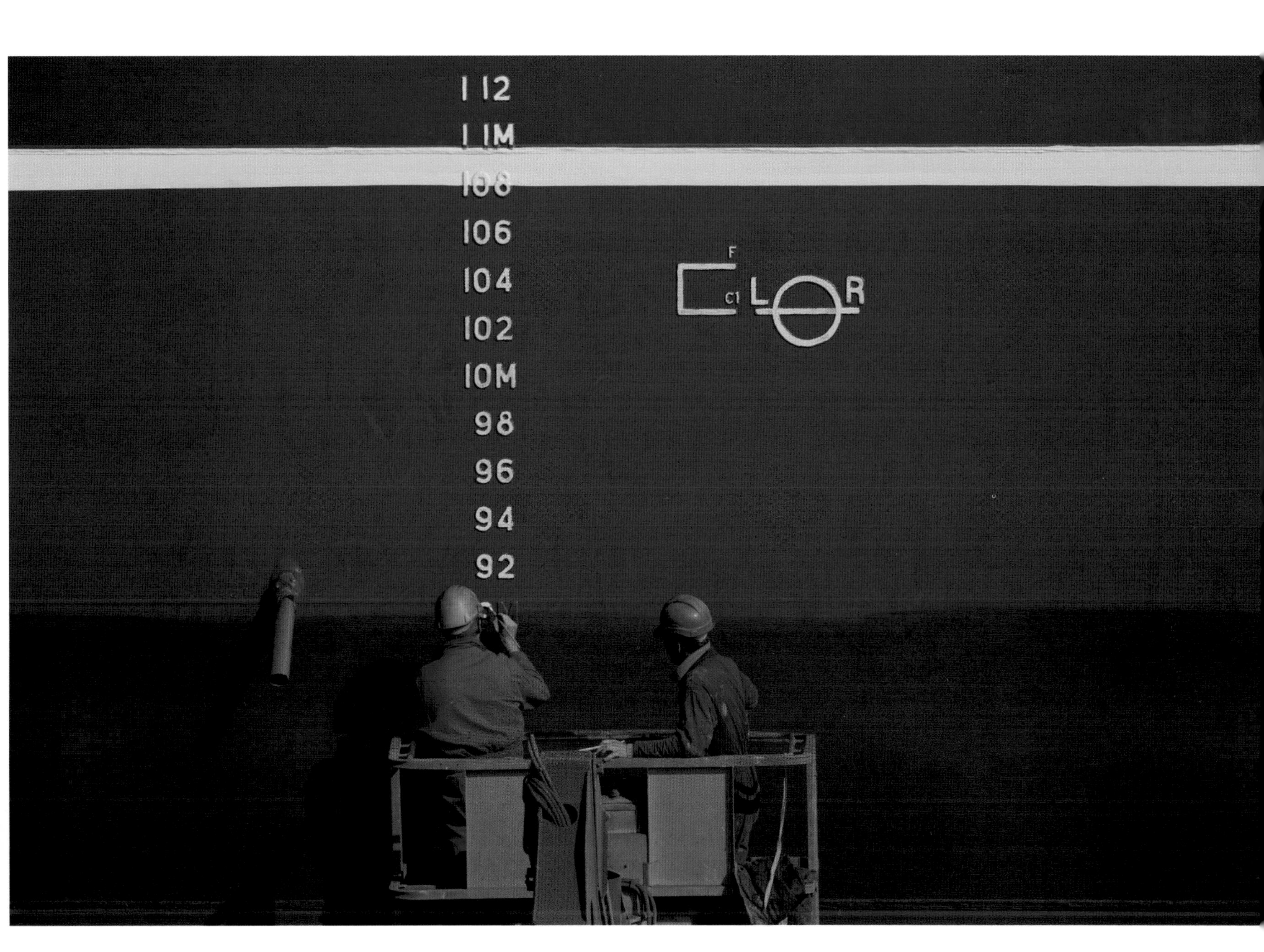

Draught markings.

Opposite:
Abseiling to apply the final touches to the funnel.

Right:
Marking the watertight bulkheads (hence the letters "WT").

Following double-page spread:
The waterline.

Final application of
anti-fouling to the stem.

Final touches of anti-fouling
to the bulbous bow.

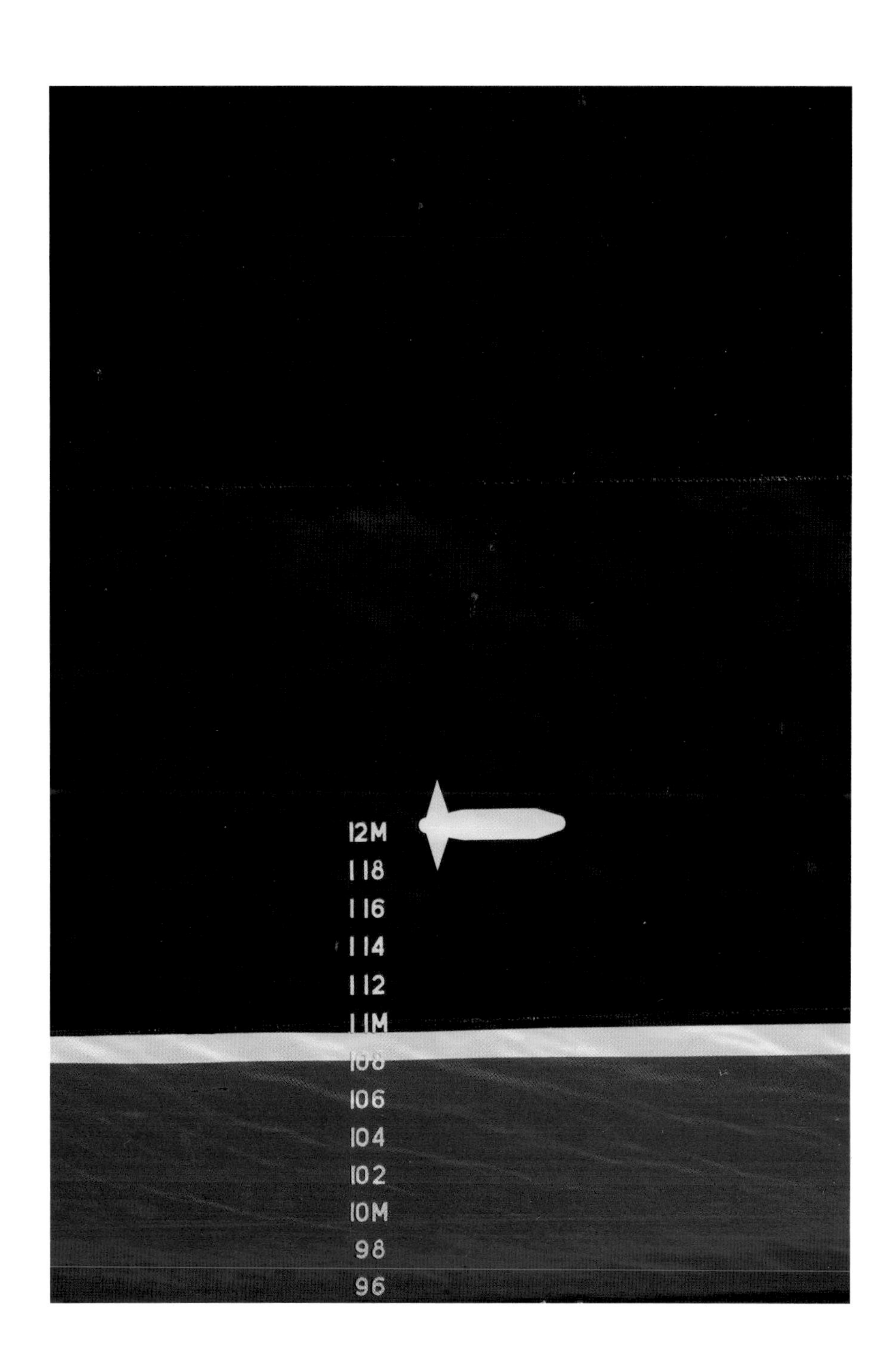

Stem and bulbous bow—
clean lines, brilliant colours.

Queen Mary 2

Final careening work before delivery to the ship-owner.

Throughout the fitting-out process, the *QM2* attracted tens of thousands of visitors, keen to get a look inside the biggest of the "château
3,000 people at work simultaneously. The interior—in the Cunard style, all soft hues—takes shape day by day, as each detail is added: d

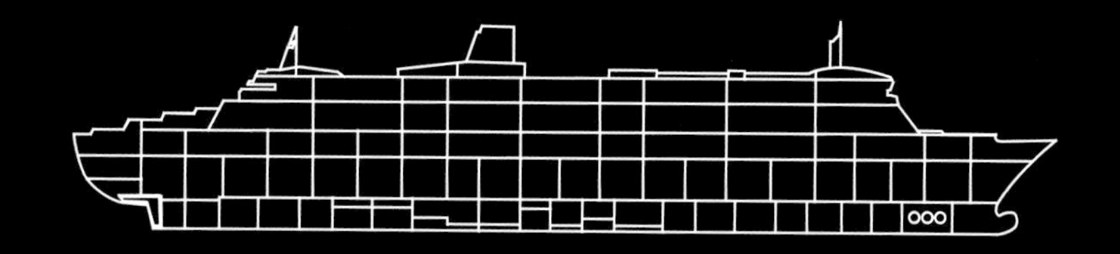

2003

THE UNVEILED

de la Loire," as the mayor of Saint-Nazaire likes to call the liners that leave the estuary. The ship looks like a veritable hive, with almost
wood fittings, thick carpets, teak decks, bas-reliefs, and glasswork.

INTERIORS

ENTREPOSE
MacGREGOR
T4280R

Opposite:
Laying the technical networks before decoration begins.

Above:
Escalators link kitchen and restaurant so that service can run as smoothly as possible.

Following double-page spread:
The carpet has already been laid in the Royal Court Theatre, which awaits its seats. It will seat 1,094 people on two levels and be equipped with the latest sound and lighting technology, a revolving platform, an orchestra pit that can be lowered or raised to increase the stage area, and a wall of images to serve as scenery.

ROCKWOOL

VIBAC

Left, top:
A welder at work looks like an astronaut in the universe of the planetarium.

Left, middle:
The casino, before the installation of the gaming tables and gambling machines.

Left, bottom:
The tiers, seen here under construction, will be able to accommodate an audience of 1,000.

Opposite:
In the ship's central artery, an artist lays gold leaf on the ceiling.

Following double-page spread:
The dome of the planetarium is designed to be lowered over the audience so that they find themselves in the centre of the galaxy. This is the first planetarium ever built on board a ship.

Opposite:
The Queen's Room: 100 square metres of dance floor in inlaid wood, under crystal chandeliers. This is the biggest ballroom at sea, taking up the entire width of the ship: its windows look out to sea on either side.

Above:
The *QM2*'s discothèque is on two floors. The designers intended to re-create the atmosphere of the shipyard (untreated platework, visible structural elements) and even named the discothèque G32—the *QM2*'s shipyard code name.

Opposite:
Luxury and refinement in the duplex apartments (top) and penthouses (bottom).

Right:
Infinite perspective along the cabin-deck gangways.

Opposite:
The panoramic lifts in the atrium or "Grand Lobby" (the *QM2*'s main entrance hall) provide access to decks 2 to 7.

Right, top:
Finishing the mouldings. These cast-plaster designs require a great deal of finishing work.

Right, bottom:
Maintenance trolley at the foot of the Grand Lobby.

GRAND
LOBBY

Laying carpets in the Grand Lobby which, like the eye of a cyclops, is at ship's centre.

GRAND
LOBBY

Opposite:
The atrium ceiling, five deck heights above the heads of those on its floor, seems to be supported by the tall columns of the panoramic lifts. A few lucky cabins will have a bird's-eye view onto this exceptional space.

Above:
Fluidity and transparency: the atrium stairs.

Following double-page spread:
Final adjustments are made to the decorated glass of the luminous dome of the Britannia restaurant, which can seat 1,374 people on two decks.

Above:
The Britannia's main staircase recalls that of the Grand Lobby. This ceremonial staircase, used for gala dinners, sweeps down to the captain's table (seen here being put in place in the background).

Opposite:
The Britannia's dome rises 40 feet (12 metres) above the floor.

Left, above:
Like a vision, the 1/100th scale model of the *QM2*, 11.5 feet (3.5 metres) long and all lit up from within, floats behind the bar in the Observation Lounge.

Left, below:
The ship's main swimming pool is on Deck 12. In good weather, the glass roof can be opened completely.

Opposite, top:
The waiting area in front of the lifts.

Opposite, bottom:
Reception desk of the College at Sea, which will host many seminars. Opposite the desk, the panel made up of period documents is just a small part of the great mural that runs along all the *QM2*'s gangways, telling the story of Cunard from its beginnings.

EXIT

On 22 December 2003, at about 3:30 P. M., two years after the start of construction, forty years after the *France*, and seventy years after the
to see the launch of the first liner of the twenty-first century. The *Queen Mary 2* then changes flags, becoming a British ship and joining

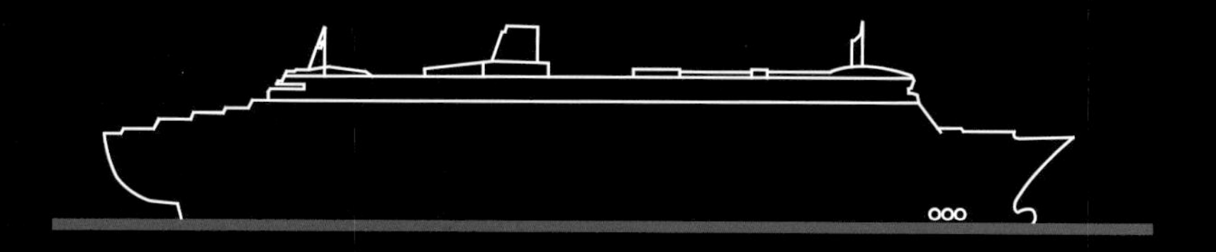

22/12/2003

THE FAREWELLS IN SAINT-NAZAIRE

Normandie, the *Queen Mary 2* leaves the port of Saint-Nazaire for good. Tens of thousands of people crowd the coast, despite the freezing
the glorious Cunard fleet. The queen of England will officially name her on 8 January 2004.

22 December 2003, 9:45 A. M.: the announcement that the purchase of the *QM2* has been finally signed by the ship-owner rings out over the ship's decks. Hundreds of workers bid farewell to the queen of the seas, where almost 17,000 people have worked side by side for almost two years.

P 218

Captain Ron Warwick, the first commander of the *Queen Mary 2*. His father, commodore W. E. Warwick, was the first captain of the *Queen Elizabeth 2*.

CUNARD

Queen Mary

The *QM2*'s four whistles sound in the fog. She is about to sail.

Following double-page spread:
The tugboats and navy vessels set off their water pumps in a gesture of farewell.

In perfect formation, the eight aircraft of the Patrouille de France appear on the horizon to salute the departure of the *QM2* with a blue, white, and red trail.

EE OUEST

A final message from the departing *Queen*.

The course is set for Southampton.

AT SEA
THE FIRST MONTHS OF NAVIGATION

01-02-03/2004

January, February, and March 2004. For her first three months in operation, the *Queen Mary 2* will sail the Caribbean. During this time her home port will be Fort Lauderdale, Florida.

Opposite:
Early in the morning, the first tenders take to the water (one can be seen on the port side) to allow passengers to go ashore, where they can join excursions to the islands.

Left:
Those who do not want to go ashore can enjoy the sunshine by one of the two swimming pools on the quarter deck.

February 2004. The *QM2* at anchor, a few cable lengths from Roseau (Dominica).

Queen Mary 2

Dominica Lotteries
Commission
LOTTO
WIN LOTTO
DAILY 3
Instant Money
Games
Tel. No : 449 8500
Hotline : 447 2500
" You've Got To Be
In It To Win It "
LOTTO 50000
WIN LOTTO 650000

Following double-page spread:
View from Scotts Head, south of Roseau.

Queen Mary 2
CUNARD

Slipping between islands on the way to her next port of call, the *QM2* turns on her lights in the warm evening.

Following double-page spread:
February 2004, early morning. The *QM2* manoeuvres herself to the quayside in the port of Fort-de-France (Martinique). In the foreground, the Pointe-Nègre lighthouse.

In port at Fort-de-France.

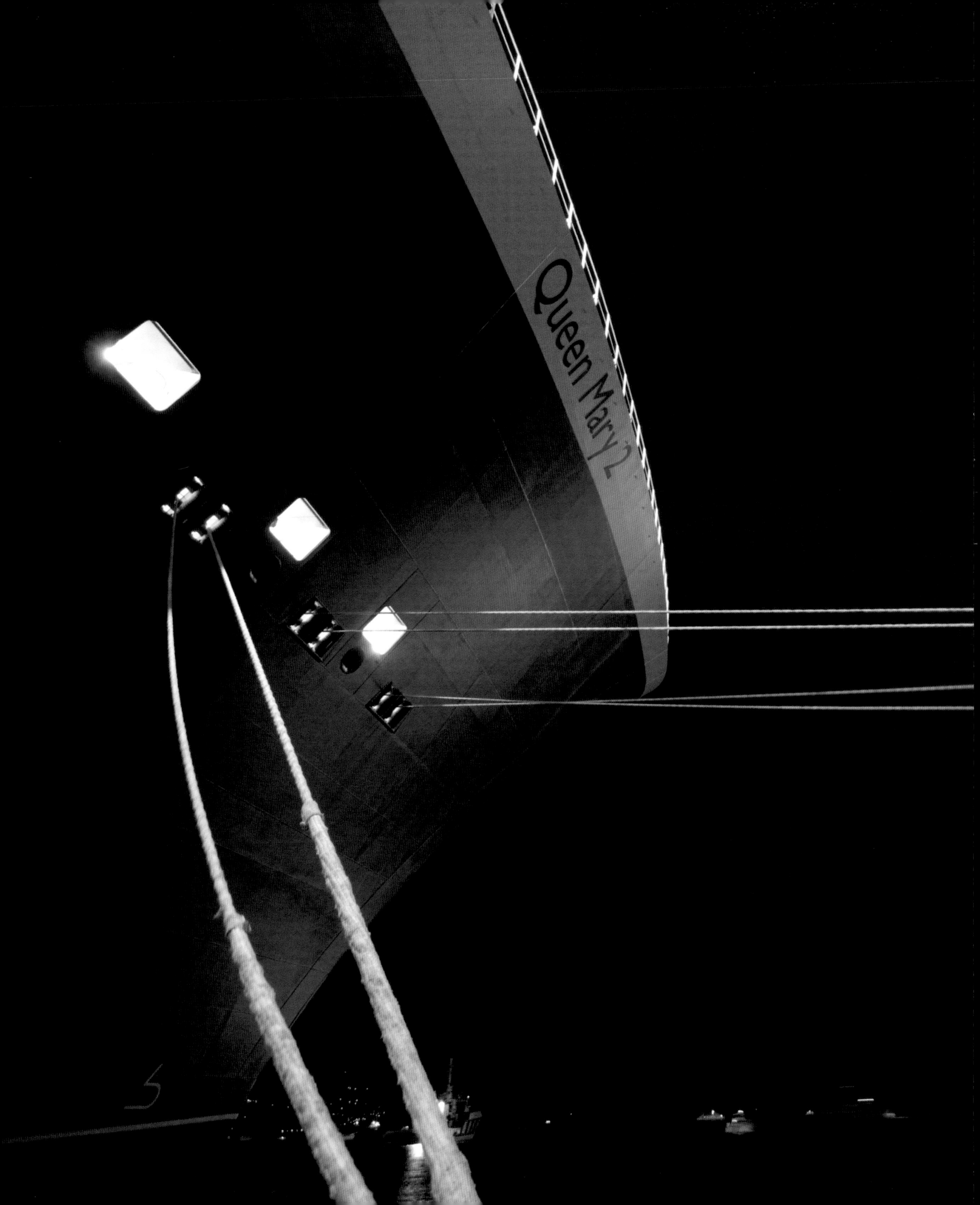
Queen Mary 2

Left:
Fireworks from the citadel of Fort-de-France salute the *QM2*'s arrival.

Following double-page spread:
The extraordinary party laid on by the people of Martinique for the *QM2* continued until she finally left. This was Martinique's way of paying tribute to her son, Jean-Rémy Villageois, who directed the construction of the *QM2* at Saint-Nazaire.

Queen
CUNARD

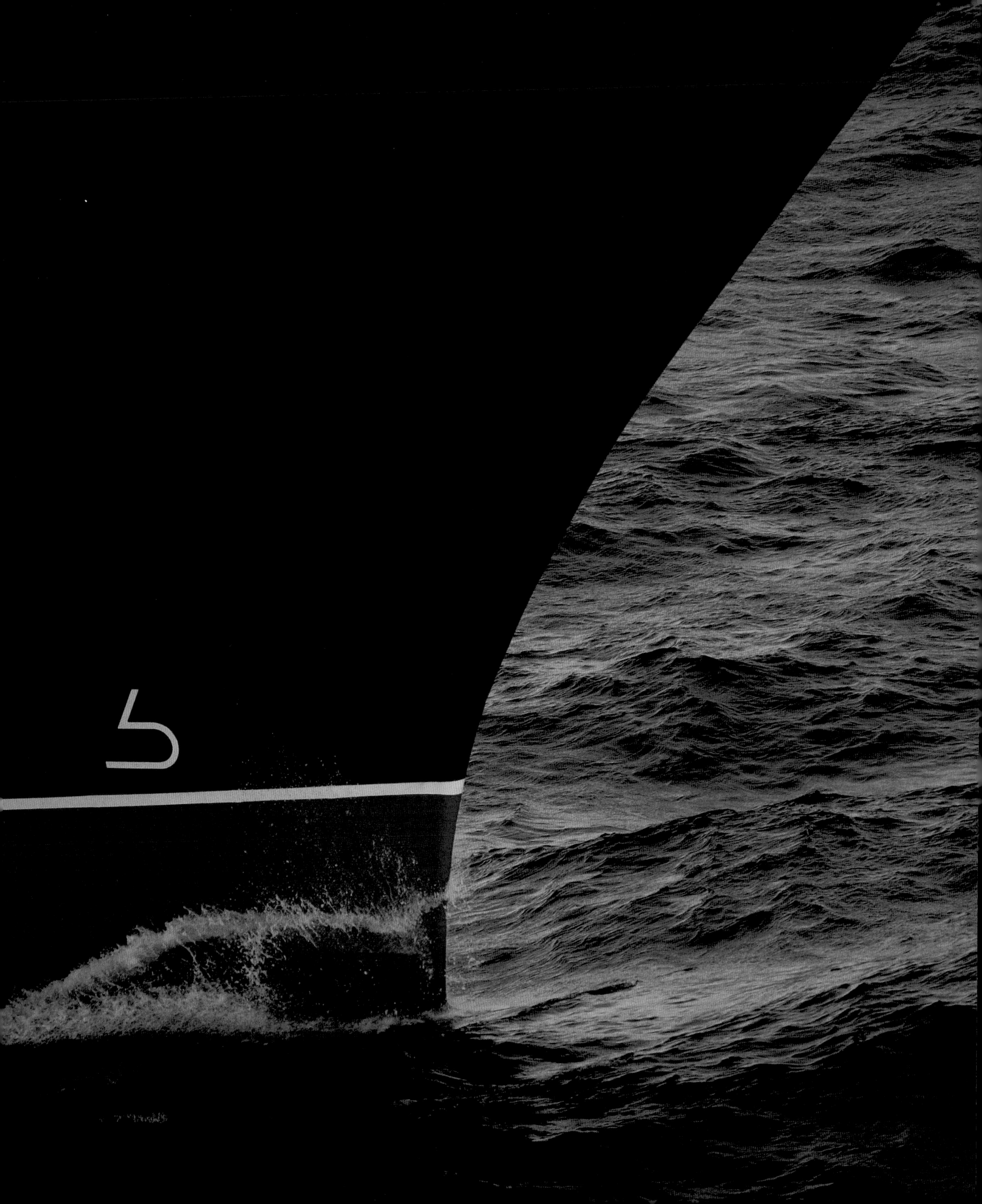

SOUTHAMPTON–NEW YORK
INAUGURAL CROSSING

16-22/04/2004

16 April 2004. Setting off on the inaugural crossing of the legendary Southampton/New York route, which will take six days.

Right:
The ship leaves Southampton, saluted by tugs.

Opposite:
Safety drill before departure. Passengers prepare their life-jackets.

Following double-page spreads:
Heading for the open ocean.

AURORA
1-3-5

CUNARD
Queen Mary 2

Queen Mary 2
CUNARD

The very early morning is unquestionably the best time to enjoy being on board ship. There is no one, or almost no one, on the decks or in the Jacuzzis. One feels as if one has the ship to oneself.

The little balconies of the quarter deck are wonderful lookouts for seeing the whole length of the *QM2* and her bow-wave.

As the *QM2* heads west, the quarter deck is bathed in sunlight all morning.

Heading due west, the rising sun is exactly in line with the ship's wake. The first group activity of the day is a gymnastics lesson on the quarter deck.

OCEAN LINERS IN THE WORLD

$515.42
HAYWIRE
25¢
THIS MACHINE ACCEPTS

Above:
After the first seating, passengers can visit the planetarium or the Royal Court Theatre (above), where a different performance takes place every evening. The angle of inclination of the large chandelier indicates the state of the sea. On this crossing, an evening performance was cancelled because of an exceptionally violent storm.

Opposite:
8 P. M. The second seating begins in the Britannia.

Every evening, a great ball is held in the Queen's Room, with an orchestra playing all the great classics one after the other. Cunard has even laid on "escorts" who invite unaccompanied women—or those whose husbands don't care to dance—on to the ballroom floor. The architects and interior designers named the discothèque G32, the *QM2*'s code name at Chantiers de l'Atlantique. There, passengers can dance into the small hours, whatever the weather, to the rock hits of the 1960s

QM2
QM2

← 22-20-18-16
14-12-10-8-6-4-2 →

A change in latitude and longitude. There is an area of low pressure in the North Atlantic. Passengers should dress accordingly, but on Deck 7 they can still enjoy the 360-degree, 2,000-foot (600-metre) promenade deck.

Curiously, everyone walks round the promenade deck in the same direction—anticlockwise—even though there are no instructions to do so.

The area of low pressure is here at last, with force 11 winds and waves 33 to 46 feet (10 to 14 metres) high.

Only large ships more than 985 feet (300 metres) long can keep up their speed in a storm: because they are longer than the wavelength of the sea, they barely toss in the water. During this extremely violent storm, only two waves really shook the *QM2*'s stem. On arrival in New York, Captain Warwick admitted to passengers that he had never experienced such an area of low pressure in the North Atlantic.

When the *QM2* travels at such high speed through a North Atlantic depression, she heads rapidly north-west. The force of the waves thus hits her from the side, and the quality and efficiency of the stabilisers can be fully appreciated.

Still farther west, arrival on the Banks of Newfoundland, whose legendary fog shrouds the ship. Visibility is zero. Nevertheless, the vessel continues to travel at 30 knots, and it is essential to be extra vigilant, for a collision at such a speed would be disastrous. The crew do not take their eyes off the stem and the radar screens, and Captain Warwick does not leave the bridge for the twenty-four hours the fog lasts.

22 April 2004, 7 A. M.
The long-awaited moment
is here at last: Liberty Island
can be seen in the distance.

P 284

P 285

The first sight of America: a dazzling spectacle, fully up to the passengers' expectations.

Old Europe salutes the New World.

Following double-page spread:
As passengers marvel at the view, the voice of Frank Sinatra resounds on deck in "New York, New York."

Final manoeuvres at the quayside.

Following double-page spread:
Twelfth Avenue: a prestigious address for two days in port.

EXIT

COAST-TO-COAST
IN UNDER A SECOND.

Queen Mary 2

Opposite:
25 April 2004. *The Queen Elizabeth 2* has joined the *Queen Mary 2* for a special crossing: both Cunard flagships will sail side by side for Southampton.

W YORKER
MACYS

Queen Mary 2

CUNARD: HISTORY OF A SHIP COMPANY

CUNARD: HISTORY OF A SHIP COMPANY

Cunard is a famous name. It may have been more famous fifty years ago, when it ranked alongside Harrods in terms of recognition, and even people who had never seen a ship could name the captain of the *Queen Mary*. But even now, long after the era of ocean travel that established its fame, Cunard remains a magnificently evocative name, synonymous with grandiose saloons, film stars, and impeccable service worthy of a great palace.

Even more remarkably, the great liners associated with the Cunard name are all equally famous. Who has not heard of the *Queen Elizabeth*? Or the *Mauretania*? Or the most famous transatlantic liner afloat today, *Queen Elizabeth 2*? The *Titanic* stands almost alone—excepting the *France* and the *Normandie*—as a ship of legendary fame that did not fly the Cunard house flag.

Samuel Cunard, Pioneer

Back in 1839, as he contemplated setting up the company, Samuel Cunard would have been astonished to learn of the eventual fame his name would achieve, never mind the fact that it would be identified as quintessentially British and synonymous with a sybaritic lifestyle. The company's longevity—163 years—would have surprised his contemporaries even more, especially those who judged Cunard's ambitions to be excessive and passed over the opportunity to join his shipping venture.

Samuel Cunard, a Halifax businessman, before he founded his company (1830s)

Strangest of all is that a man like Cunard could have formed the company in the first place. The gamble, the risk, the sheer boldness of the plan stood in sharp contrast to the character of the man. Unremittingly prudent, conservative, cautious, austere—and aged well over fifty—this Canadian of U.S. parentage hardly seemed suited to the huge economic and technological risks entailed in the founding of this company.

By the time he came to set up the British and North American Royal Mail Steam Packet Company, as Cunard's company was originally known, Samuel Cunard was already a prosperous businessman and a significant figure in the Canadian province of Nova Scotia. He was comfortably settled, with his children around him, and at an age by which most people in those days were already dead. A comfortable retirement in the cosy glow of local esteem, and not the creation of a commercial revolution, seemed to lie ahead.

Yet in 1839, Cunard gambled everything he had to set up a transatlantic ship service 3,000 miles from home—barely two years after the first Atlantic crossing by a steamship (the Irish vessel *Sirius*). He even uprooted himself from his native Nova Scotia and took up residence in London.

This drastic action was in complete contrast with everything Cunard had done before, and with everything he did afterwards, once the company was up and running and its conservatism was established (in the mould of its founder).

What originally sparked Cunard's interest was an advertisement in the *Times*. Placed by the British Admiralty—at that time responsible for carrying the mail overseas—it invited tenders from steamship owners for the provision of a timetabled steamship service to carry the Royal Mail between Britain and North America. A contract of £55,000 a year was offered. The spur for the admiralty's apparent generosity was the extraordinarily unreliable mail service provided by sailing ships: timetables were random, a transatlantic crossing took at least six weeks, departure dates were irregular, and arrival dates even more so. It was therefore never known when the mail would arrive nor even, given the frequent shipwrecks, whether it would arrive at all. What the admiralty wanted, in line with the new mechanized technology of the Victorian age, was a maritime equivalent of the railway, still brand new and remarkable for its timetables.

Unable to find Canadian partners for what must have seemed a foolhardy venture, Cunard submitted his successful bid after the admiralty's deadline, without sufficient finance, with no steamships, and with very little knowledge of the project's technical requirements. Nonetheless, his bid was successful. Unlike his competitors, whose tenders told the admiralty what they should have instead of bidding on the basis of what was asked for, Cunard's bid was austere and straightforward. He offered simply to provide the required service for the sum offered. He then went on to sign a contract with potentially ruinous clauses—£15,000 payable for any cancelled sailing, and £500 for each day a ship was late. What madness was this?

Cunard still managed to find his financial backing in Scotland and Liverpool. After having ordered four ships—each twice as big as he'd originally intended—he found himself in a position of strength, able to renegotiate the contract to his advantage.

Cunarders in Dickens's Time

Cunard's first ship, the 1,156-ton *Britannia*, left Liverpool on 4 July 1840 with Cunard himself on board; she arrived exactly on schedule in Halifax just ten days later. Within a year, *Britannia* and her three sister ships were providing a timetabled weekly steamship service across the Atlantic—the first ever. Cunard's first ships were far removed from the luxury associated with the name today. Plain, practical, and sturdy, they were as unostentatious as possible. Cabins were small—"like a hearse," wrote Dickens, who travelled on *Britannia* in 1842—each divided from the next by a partition, atop which sat a shared candle. There was a single wooden bunk, a straw mattress, and a small cupboard. Passengers were responsible for washing their own plates and cutlery, though eating was often far from their minds in inclement weather as they paddled about below decks ankle-deep in water. "There's water pouring down the stairs," exclaimed one early passenger to an officer. "We only worry, madam," he replied calmly "when it's coming *up* the stairs." Fresh meat ran out early in each voyage, after which salted beef was all that was available, and milk was supplied by a hapless cow slung on the deck in a hammock.

The *Britannia*, the first Cunarder, was steam-powered and driven by paddle wheels. Charles Dickens sailed on her.

Uncomfortable and basic though they were, Cunard's steamships nevertheless had two great advantages over sailing ships. First, they got the agony over more quickly—ten days as opposed to six weeks—and second, they were steadfastly safe and reliable.

Cunard himself made safety his priority. To this day, the Cunard company has never been responsible for the loss of a single passenger or a single mailbag on the Atlantic run. Cunard's original instruction to his first master, Captain Woodroffe, was simple: "Speed is nothing; safety is all that is required." The company has followed that motto religiously ever since, even in later years, when competition became heated for the Blue Riband. Cunard ships have held the coveted prize for over sixty-one years. However, when a trophy was made in the 1930s in recognition of the regularised record, Sir Percy Bates—then chairman of Cunard—refused to accept it, despite *Queen Mary* being the current holder.

Cunard's safety and reliability record was such that passengers would refuse to board other lines' ships, insisting instead on waiting for the next Cunarder. Naturally, this reputation made Cunard profits.

Battle in the North Atlantic

The company's first excursion into war brought a serious threat to that prosperity. In 1854, fourteen Cunard ships—almost the entire fleet—were requisitioned for the Crimean War. While the company's contribution to the war effort was remarkable, including the transport of all the horses that charged with the Light Brigade, all Cunard mail services across the Atlantic stopped. The American Collins Line, heavily subsidised by the U.S. government, won Cunard's lucrative business by default. Crimea gave Samuel Cunard a baronetcy, but it gave Collins a monopoly on the Atlantic.

However, over-expansion and a cavalier attitude to safety did Collins in. Despite being subsidised at twice the value of Cunard's mail contract, Collins went bankrupt in 1858. Cunard regained its preeminence.

Samuel Cunard's innate conservatism flared up again in the late 1850s, when he steadfastly refused to contemplate the change from paddle wheels to propellers—despite the latter's obvious superiority. He only relented in 1862, with the construction of the *China*.

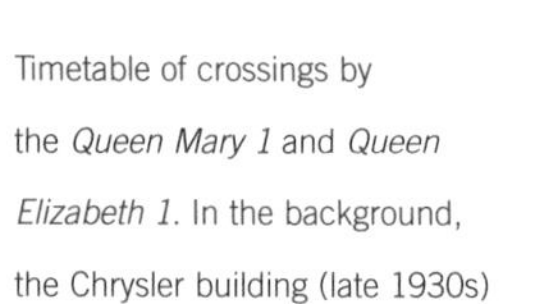

Timetable of crossings by the *Queen Mary 1* and *Queen Elizabeth 1*. In the background, the Chrysler building (late 1930s)

Timetable for Southampton—New York crossings by the *Mauretania*, holder at the time of the Blue Riband (c. 1910)

The *China*, which had been built to cater specifically to emigrants, heralded the decline of mail-transport work. And so emigration became Cunard's next guarantee of prosperity. Between 1860 and 1900, almost 14 million people emigrated from Europe to the United States; of those, 4.5 million passed through Liverpool, with half setting sail on Cunard vessels. Cunard's next challenge was the introduction of the "floating hotel," spearheaded by the newly formed British company White Star's *Oceanic* in 1870. Where *Oceanic* had bathtubs and taps, Cunard offered basins and jugs; where *Oceanic* had central heating, Cunard passengers had to make do with stoves; where *Oceanic* had lamps, Cunard offered candles; and where *Oceanic* had lavatories, Cunard managed with chamber pots.

Falling passenger numbers forced Cunard not only to follow suit but to innovate. The *Servia* of 1881 was the first steel Cunarder, the first to be built with an electricity supply, the first to have bathrooms en suite and—interestingly—the first whose budget relied solely on passenger revenue. Henceforth, mail was to play a marginal role.

The *Carpathia*, *Mauretania*, *Lusitania*, and Others

The year 1902 saw the virtually unnoticed launch on the Tyne of a minor Cunarder destined for the Mediterranean trade—and also destined to become, inadvertently, one of the most famous ships of all time. She was the 13,600-tonne *Carpathia* which, on an April night in 1912, made history under the command of Captain Arthur Rostron when she sped through ice fields in the night, without the benefit of modern radar and at a speed greater than she was supposedly capable of, to rescue all the survivors of the *Titanic*. Captain Rostron, later master of the *Queen Mary* and knighted by the king, modestly remarked later that a hand greater than his own guided the little ship that night.

But that was glory yet to come; as *Carpathia* entered service, Cunard was in trouble, with an ageing transatlantic fleet facing ferocious competition from the Germans and Americans. The company fought back by launching three of its most famous ships—*Lusitania*, *Mauretania*, and *Aquitania*, true "floating palaces" that could travel at unprecedented speed. The *Mauretania* held the Blue Riband for twenty-two years. With the outbreak of World War I, the British government requisitioned most of the company's ships. During the four long years of carnage, Cunard ships transported over a million men, served as hospital ships, prisoner-of-war ships, food and munitions carriers, and as armed merchant cruisers. It was in the last role that the *Carmania* took the first German casualty of the war when she sank the *Cap Trafalgar*—ironically disguised as *Carmania*—off South America in November 1914.

Campania, meanwhile, was equipped with a 240-foot (73-metre) platform, making her the forerunner of today's aircraft carriers.

Cunard lost twenty-two ships in all, including the unrequisitioned *Lusitania*, torpedoed by a U20 submarine off the Irish coast in 1915 with the loss of 1,200 civilian lives.

The interwar years saw the company regain confidence, especially because the former German vessel *Imperator*, renamed *Berengaria*, was added to the fleet as part of war reparations.

The period was so lucrative for Cunard that the company failed to notice the significance of Charles Lindbergh's transatlantic flight in 1927. Nevertheless, the company had already begun to diversify its sources of revenue in 1921, when *Laconia* undertook the first world cruise.

No. 534—A Ghost Ship

In 1928, Cunard began the construction of a liner that George V himself was to call "the stateliest ship now in being." Admired by all, even those who had never set foot on her, this ship was to embody the pride, the triumphs, and the tribulations of an entire nation.

Cunard's intention in 1928 had been simply to replace its ageing transatlantic fleet with a new pair of steamships that could provide a weekly service in each direction, and so counter increasingly ambitious German competition in the North Atlantic. When the first of the pair, No. 534, later to be named *Queen Mary*, was revealed to be the largest and most powerful ship ever built, the chairman of Cunard, Sir Percy Bates, merely declared that she was "the smallest and slowest ship which could accomplish such a service."

Work on No. 534 began late in 1930 at the yard of John Brown and Co., on Clydebank, Scotland, with an estimated budget of £6.5m and without state aid (unlike other ship companies, which were partly financed by subsidies). However, with the coming of the Depression, passenger numbers plummeted, and Cunard's revenues fell from £9m in 1928 to less than £4m in 1931. Despite staff on shore and at sea taking a pay cut, work on the construction of *Queen Mary* stopped just before Christmas 1931.

Immediately, 3,640 men in Clydebank—a town where half the working population was employed on the *Queen Mary*—were thrown out of work. But the ripples were felt by 10,000 ancillary workers farther away. They were felt in Stoke-on-Trent, with its 200,000 pieces of crockery; in Sheffield, where 100,000 items of cutlery were being crafted; in Walsall, which was producing 400 tonness of tubes; in Rugby, manufacturing seven turbogenerators; in Liverpool, producing 8,200 square feet (762 square metres) of toughened glass; in Millwall, casting four 20-foot (6-metre) propellers; in Darlington, forging the 190-tonne stern frame; in Belfast, working on the 5.5-tonne gear wheels; in Halifax, weaving 10 miles (16 kilometres) of blankets; in St Albans, assembling 600 clocks; and in other towns up and down the land making curtains, carpets, anchor chains, and furniture. Overnight, all of them stopped.

TOP: Poster from the 1930s inviting the traveller to discover 'America this year, on board the *Queen Mary 1*'

BOTTOM: Poster showing the three funnels of the *Queen Mary 1*

The rusting skeleton of *Queen Mary*, with 80 percent of the hull rivets in place and £1.5m already spent, was symbolic of the financial catastrophe that hit the Western world. This graphic symbol was so telling that members of the public sent thousands of unsolicited donations of money to Cunard in an effort to get the work restarted. The government was implored to lend Cunard the capital to complete the ship and get people back to work, but the government steadfastly refused—until 1934, that is. In a complex deal which required Cunard to take over the running of White Star's ailing transatlantic fleet, Neville Chamberlain, then chancellor of the exchequer, agreed to lend Cunard sufficient funds to complete *Queen Mary* and build her sister ship, *Queen Elizabeth*.

Queen Mary, Flagship of Cunard White Star

On 3 April 1934, the John Brown workforce returned to work, led by the Dalmuir Pipe Band. They began by removing 130 tonnes of rust and dozens of crows' nests.

Just five months later, Queen Mary, wife of King George V, became the first monarch to launch a merchant ship. She accomplished the job with a bottle of Australian wine, which was then deemed more patriotic than the traditional French champagne. As she said the words, "I name this ship *Queen Mary*; may God bless her and all who sail in her," millions of British subjects heard her voice, broadcast over the radio, for the first time.

Watching the launch were 200,000 spectators. Many who stood on the opposite bank of the dredged and widened Clyde were thoroughly soaked by the 8-foot (2.5 metre) wave that surged across the river when the enormous hull entered the water.

A popular story has it that Cunard's board had not intended to name the ship *Queen Mary*, but, instead, planned to stick to the traditional 'ia' endings prevalent among the Cunard transatlantic fleet. They despatched one of their members, Lord Royden, to ask his friend the king for permission to name the ship *Queen Victoria*. Allegedly, Lord Royden didn't ask directly but intimated that Cunard would like to name the ship after "England's most illustrious queen." "My wife will be delighted," replied King George. "I will go and tell her now."

A good story—but not true. Cunard had already decided that since the White Star and Cunard transatlantic fleets had been combined under the new banner Cunard White Star, neither the traditional White Star 'ic' ending nor Cunard's 'ia' was appropriate. The first ship of the new company needed a name to break with tradition, and *Queen Mary* it was intended to be.

BOTTOM: The *Queen Elizabeth 1* is launched (1938).

TOP: US troops set sail for Europe on board the *Queen Mary 1* during the Second World War.

On 27 May 1936, at Southampton, *Queen Mary* cast off to the sounds of bands and ecstatic crowds and began her maiden voyage. On board were the famous bandleader Henry Hall, scheduled to give a series of live radio broadcasts during the crossing; the virtuoso harmonica player Larry Adler; and a well-known singer of the time, Frances Day, who performed *Somewhere at Sea*, a song Henry Hall had written specially for *Queen Mary*. Much as she may have liked being at sea, Miss Day did not trust the ship's eggs to be fresh by the end of the voyage, so she took along her own hens.

The rapturous welcome in New York on 1 June 1936 marked the start of four years of glamorous transatlantic service, during which *Queen Mary* won the Blue Riband twice for the fastest Atlantic crossing.

Faster than Torpedoes

Queen Elizabeth, the sister ship to *Queen Mary*, had a less glorious start. She was launched in 1938 by Queen Elizabeth, wife of George VI. The growing pressures of impending war kept the king in London. Instead, the "queen" was by then Princess Elizabeth—the present queen—and Princess Margaret.

As fitting-out work progressed, it was decided that *Queen Elizabeth* was not only a target for German air attacks, but she was also occupying Clydeside shipyard space required for the war effort. She had to move.

The captain put to sea with workmen still on board. Once out of the Clyde, he opened his sealed orders, which he expected to instruct him to go to Southampton; instead, he was told to head immediately and at full speed for New York. The secret dash was done with the launching gear still affixed to the underside of the ship, and without proper fitments inside. Men who expected to be going home within days by train from Southampton did not get home for years.

After trooping from Australia, *Queen Mary* and *Queen Elizabeth* began bringing American GIs across to Europe in 1942, at full speed and unescorted. Not only were they faster than the U boats, whose crews Hitler had offered £100,000 for sinking either of them, they were faster even than the torpedoes. In summer, 15,000 soldiers were carried on each voyage—such a huge number that the men had to sleep in shifts and observe a strict one-way traffic system on board. *Queen Mary*'s master, Commodore Sir James Bisset, noted that the ship was so difficult to handle under such circumstances that several times he was concerned for her stability. All told, she made twenty-eight such trips, taking soldiers eastbound and prisoners-of-war westbound, with *Queen Elizabeth* undertaking a similar number. On three occasions, as Sir Winston Churchill crossed the Atlantic to see President Roosevelt, *Queen Mary* was the nerve-centre of the British Empire. According to Churchill, the trooping record of the two ships, together with *Aquitania*, reduced the duration of the war by at least a year.

To Cape Horn. . .by Bus

Queen Mary and *Queen Elizabeth* enjoyed a golden period after the war, doing what they were built to do. This was the era of film stars and royalty, who were photographed by hordes of press photographers as they stepped ashore in Southampton or New York. In 1958, however, the ghost of that Lindbergh flight caught up with Cunard: for the first time, more people had crossed the Atlantic by air than by sea. The end was in sight.

Queen Mary left New York for the last time on 22 September 1967—voyage number 1,001—just two days after the queen launched *Queen Elizabeth* 2. During the crossing, the new liner passed *Queen Elizabeth* for the last time, just a mile distant, at a combined speed of 60 knots.

Having carried 2,114,000 passengers, plus 810,730 military personnel, 19,000 GI brides, and 4,000 child evacuees, and having travelled 3,794,017 nautical miles, *Queen Mary* left on her last journey from Southampton, her home port, on 31 October 1967, bound for her present home in Long Beach, California. On board were two double-decker London buses, and passengers delighted in rounding Cape Horn on a bus. She arrived to an ecstatic welcome in Long Beach, where she remains today: one of the most prestigious ships of all time is now a hotel and museum, permanently moored at the quayside.

Queen Elizabeth ended her career just a year later in an ignominious fashion, just as she had started it in less triumphant circumstances than *Queen Mary*. Sold by Cunard in 1968, she eventually ended up in Hong Kong to undergo conversion into a floating university.

There, in 1972, a number of mysterious fires broke out simultaneously. Inundated by millions of gallons of water from fire hoses, the ship turned over and sank. The sale of *Queen Mary* and *Queen Elizabeth* was the nadir in Cunard's fortunes. Toward the end, the ships had been criss-crossing the Atlantic virtually empty—on one voyage, *Queen Elizabeth* carried only 200 passengers.

The *QE2*—A Born Fighter

Though all economic indicators were unfavourable, and though the company had just pensioned off two prestigious ships which had been defeated by the jet aircraft, the Cunard board was planning to construct another transatlantic liner—an apparent act of pure madness, worthy of the company's founder.

And so *Queen Elizabeth* 2 was launched by the queen in 1967. A true transatlantic liner, she boasted a service speed of 28.5 knots and a hull 1.48 inches (3.81 centimetres) thick. Still, with her ability to navigate both the Panama and the Suez canal, the *Queen Elizabeth* 2 was the quintessential cruise ship, too. As a result of intense press speculation about her name, secret to the last, *Queen Elizabeth* 2 was already famous by the time she slid down the slipway. ("Sir Winston Churchill" and "Princess Anne" had been among the bookie's favourites). Ever since, she has remained the most famous ship in the world.

QE2—as she rapidly became—did not have an auspicious start. Her keel-laying in 1965 was delayed by three days, as the crane destined to put the keel in place toppled over instead. On her sea trials in 1968, recurring turbine problems were followed by a total breakdown off the Antilles, as a result of which *QE2* limped into her home port on her first call at Southampton in January 1969. Cunard refused to accept delivery, six brochured cruises were cancelled, and the maiden voyage had to be delayed until May.

If this misfortune were not gloom enough, city analysts predicted *QE2* would never make a profit and that she would be mothballed within six months—a mad adventure, the last fling of a defunct company, a white elephant.

Well, how wrong can analysts be? Thirty-four years, 2,000 crossings, 5 million miles and about 3 million passengers later, the most famous ship in the world sails serenely on—still making the profits she has turned in from the outset, still stopping the traffic on Sydney Harbour Bridge, still attracting the rich and the famous in

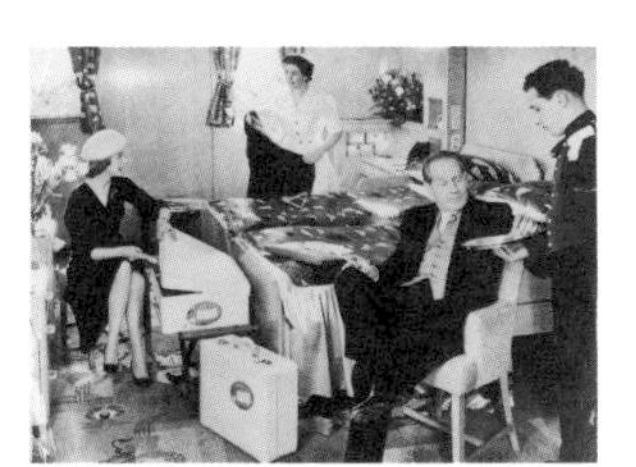

Snapshots of life on board the *Queen Mary 1*.
(FROM TOP): Passengers are greeted by luxury on board as soon as they enter their comfortable suite; unusual pastimes on the promenade deck: a game of blind-man's-buff or a boxing match; the restaurant is decorated for Christmas Eve; the swimming pool, where the elegant bathers of the 1950s relaxed and made new friends.

almost equal measure with the not-so-rich or famous: still centre stage.

And what a dramatic thirty-four years they have been. In 1972, an American extortionist threatened that unless a ransom was paid, suicide accomplices on board would blow up the *QE2* in mid-Atlantic. Although the ship already had comprehensive search routines in place, as a precaution Cunard arranged with the ministry of defence for SAS personnel to be parachuted into the sea near to *QE2*. A further search was carried out, but no explosives were found. The extortionist was caught and sentenced to twenty years in prison. Just a year later, according to Anwar Sadat, former president of Egypt, Colonel Gaddafi was making plans to torpedo *QE2* as she passed through the Mediterranean—and only Sadat's last-minute intervention prevented the attack.

As if that run of malign interest were not enough, in 1976 three members of the IRA were arrested trying to take explosives on board *QE2*.

But the ship had not finished playing her part in history. On 4 May 1982, en route to Southampton from Philadelphia, the British government requisitioned *Queen Elizabeth 2* for service in the Falklands War, and so she joined the ranks of the great Cunarders called upon to serve their country.

Reconquering the Falklands

The launch of the *Queen Elizabeth 2* (1967)

Conversion work began immediately to prepare the ship for trooping duties. Helicopter landing pads were constructed on the quarter deck and aft over the two swimming pools, with the former being particularly dangerous when the ship was travelling at speed.

Valuable paintings and furniture were removed, pipes for refuelling at sea were laid through passenger areas, and hardboard was placed over carpets. Equipment, rations, vehicles, fuel, and spare parts were loaded aboard—so much that a great deal had to be stored on the open deck.

To man the ship, Cunard asked its employees for volunteers willing to go to the war zone. It required 650; almost 1,000 applied. On 12 May 1982, 3,000 men of the Fifth Infantry Brigade came aboard, comprising units of the Scots Guards, the Welsh Guards, and Gurkha Rifles, along with naval personnel. Under the command of Captain Peter Jackson, *QE2* put to sea and headed south.

On the journey south from Freetown, the only port of call, every one of the liner's portholes was covered with black plastic to create a total blackout: from being the ocean's brightest star, *QE2*—for her own safety—became the darkest.

Ten days later, news came through of the loss of the *Atlantic Conveyor*, a Cunard ship also serving in the Falklands War. This was deeply distressing for everyone, as many of the *QE2*'s crew had friends aboard the *Atlantic Conveyor*; the news of heavy loss of life caused enormous sadness.

On the last leg of the outbound voyage, on 23 May, the navigation lights were extinguished and the radar turned off in order to silence the ship electronically. This deprived *QE2*'s navigating officers of a vital aid and put them back half a century. But the situation became particularly grave once the ship entered ice fields north of South Georgia. Huge icebergs were encountered on the night of 26 May—many bigger than the ship—and fog reduced visibility to less than a mile.

On 27 May, *QE2* anchored in Cumberland Bay, South Georgia, where the job of transferring troops and supplies to other vessels began. After this, 640 survivors of *HMS Ardent*, *Coventry*, and *Antelope* came aboard to be repatriated.

Twelve days later, and having covered 15,000 miles since first setting out from Southampton a month earlier, *Queen Elizabeth 2* was home, having carried out her mission.

Full Speed Ahead!

In 1983, conscious of *QE2*'s pulling power, Cunard decided to invest £110 million in replacing the twenty-year-old steam turbines with diesel electric engines.

On 20 October 1986, *QE2* left New York for her last-ever crossing as a steamship: *QE2*'s last and Cunard's last.

Cunard had been the first company to offer a timetabled steamship service across the Atlantic. Having survived war, depression, and foreign competitors, it was now the last to do so. But *QE2* reemerged the following year to carry on the company's tradition, with a new propulsion system and a renewed life expectancy. Conventional wisdom still maintained, however, that *QE2* would be the last transatlantic liner, and that no vessel would replace her when she was gone. Once again, the rumours proved wrong.

Among Carnival Corporation's first announcements in 1998, when it bought Cunard, was the construction of a new transatlantic liner to follow in the glorious wake of the *Britannia*, *Mauretania*, *Aquitania*, *Queen Mary*, *Queen Elizabeth*, and *QE2*.

Instead, a heritage everyone thought was bound to die lives on: the *Queen Mary 2* is indeed the triumph of a great tradition.

(FROM TOP): Queen Mary names the *Queen Mary 1*, becoming the first sovereign ever to launch a merchant navy vessel, with the words: "I name this ship *Queen Mary*; may God bless her and all who sail in her" (1934); the naming of the *Queen Mary 2* by Queen Elizabeth (2004); the *Queen Mary 2*

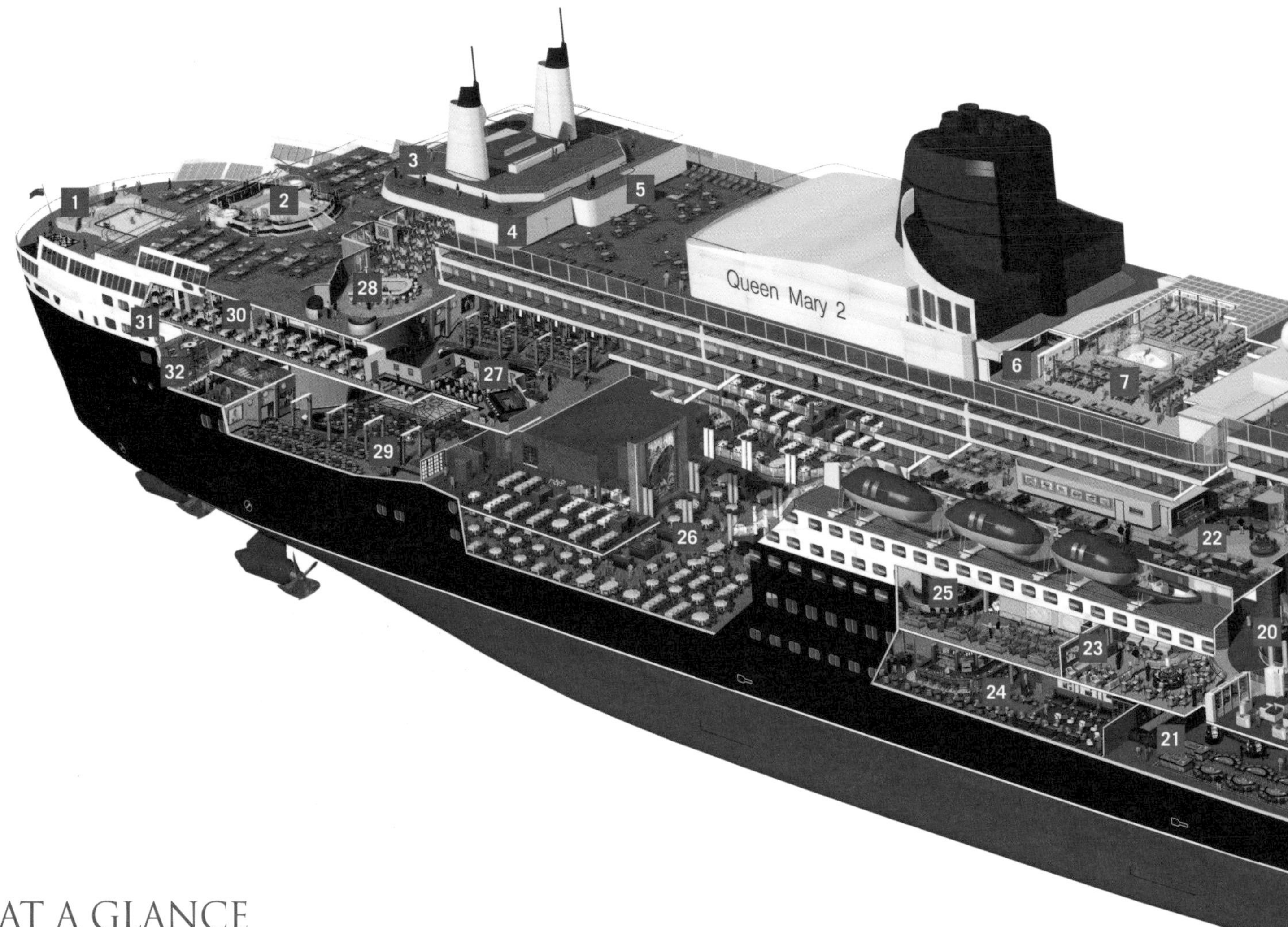

QM2 AT A GLANCE

1 Minnows Pool
2 Terrace Pool
3 Grand Duplex & Duplex Apartments
4 Kennels
5 Boardwalk Café
6 Fairways · Golf Simulators
7 The Pavilion
8 Splash Pool
9 Sports Centre
10 The Lookout · Observation Deck
11 Atlantic Room
12 Commodore Club Lounge
13 Library & Bookshop
14 Royal Suites with private lift access
15 Illuminations · Theatre & Auditorium
16 Canyon Ranch SpaClub
17 Cunard ConneXions™
18 Royal Court Theatre
19 Winter Garden
20 Grand Lobby
21 Empire Casino
22 Kings Court Alternative Dining Venues
23 Veuve Clicquot Champagne Bar
24 Golden Lion Pub
25 Chart Room Bar and Lounge
26 Britannia Restaurant
27 Queens Grill Lounge
28 Todd English Restaurant
29 Queen's Room · Ballroom
30 Queens Grill
31 Children's Facilities
32 G32 Nightclub

Mayfair Shops · Sir Samuel's Wine Bar · The Zone & Play Zone children's facilities · Princess Grill · Regatta Bar · Churchill's Cigar Lounge

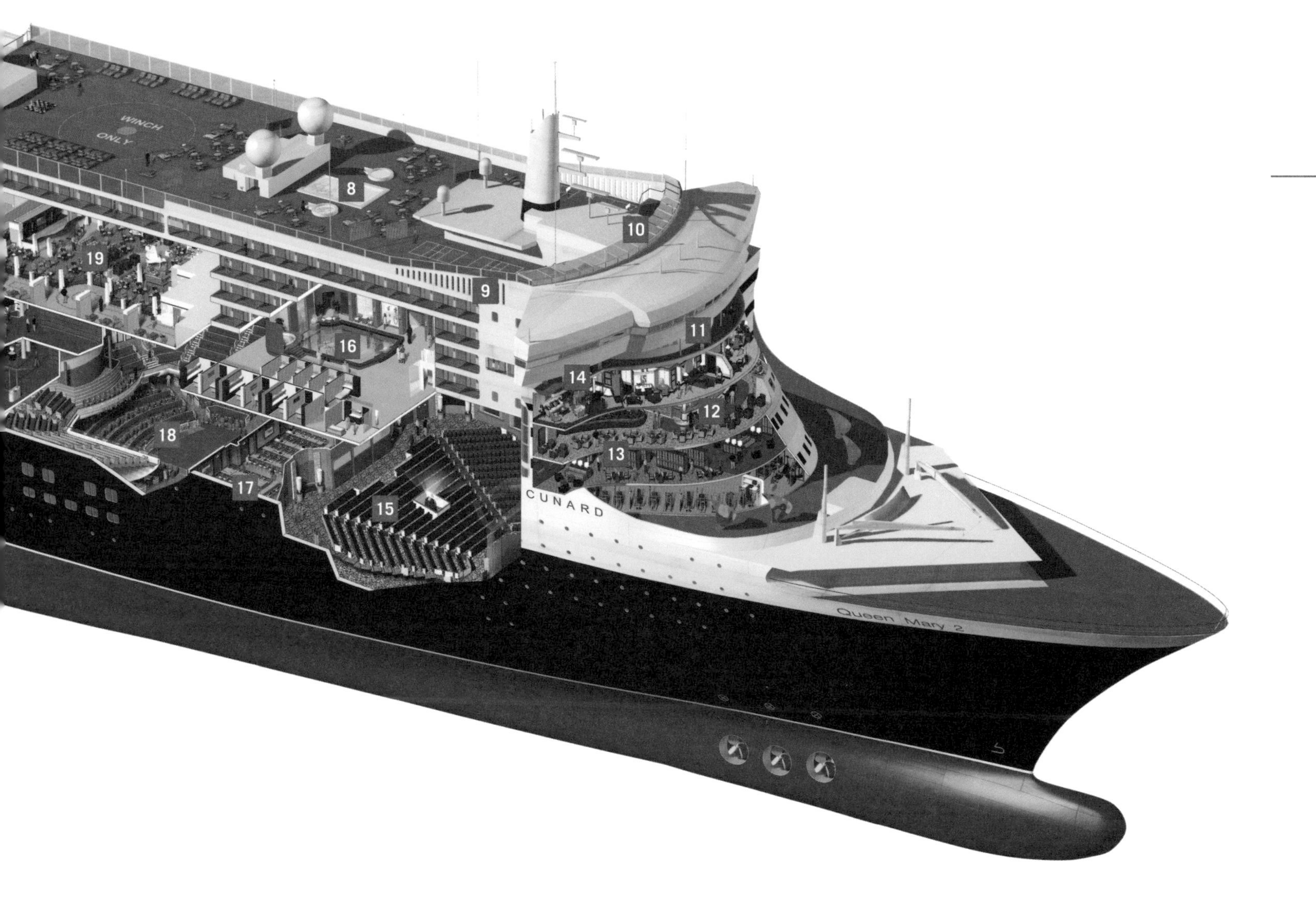
WINCH
ONLY
8
9
10
11
12
13
14
15
16
17
18
19
CUNARD
Queen Mary 2

TABLE OF CONTENTS

ABOUT THE AUTHORS

A highly acclaimed marine photographer, who in 1991 was admitted into the exclusive and historic group Peintres de la Marine (Official Painters of the French Navy), **Philip Plisson** has indulged in his passion for more than twenty-five years. His love of the sea led him in 1982 to leave the banks of the Loire and the Sologne and to settle down in La Trinité-sur-Mer, the village where he spent his vacations as a child. His work includes today more than 220,000 images and about forty books produced over the past ten years. Plisson is also the author of the captions in the "Southampton—New York Inaugural Crossing" chapter.

Working by his father's side since 1992, **Guillaume Plisson** developed a personal sensibility and eye for the profession of photography. His passion for new technology allowed him to produce audiovisual shows (for the disarmament of the aircraft-carrier *Clemenceau* and on the construction of the *Queen Mary* 2) and to be more closely involved in the interpretation of the images amassed over so many years by the Plissons, father and son.

Gwen-Haël Denigot is a freelance journalist. From her childhood in the shipbuilding town of Saint-Nazaire, she inherited a taste for ports and large ships. She is a regular collaborator of the magazine *Science & Vie*. She is the author of the three major texts at the beginning of the book.

Growing up on the northeast coast of England, **Eric Flounders** always had a passion for ships. Working some twenty years for Cunard in London, he is the author of "Cunard: History of a Ship Company."

Jean-Rémy Villageois was the project manager for the *Queen Mary* 2 at Chantiers de l'Atlantique. In charge of the engineering during the first months of study, he then took on the complete responsibility of the project up until the delivery of the transatlantic liner to Cunard. He is the author of the captions in the "Construction" chapter.

ACKNOWLEDGMENTS

We would like to thank all the participants in this wonderful adventure: The workers, staff, executives, engineers, and subcontractors of Alstom Chantiers de l'Atlantique, most particularly to: Patrick Boissier, President and Chief Executive Officer of Alstom Chantiers de l'Atlantique, Philippe Kasse, Communications Officer, Jean-Rémy Villageois, Chief Engineer for the *QM2*, Bernard Biger, of the Audiovisual Service, Jean-Paul Peignet, and Isabelle Huyghe. A great thank-you goes to Cunard for their hospitality and collaboration. Thanks to: Micky Arison, Chairman of the Board and Chief Executive Officer of the Carnival Corporation, Pamela Conover, President and Chief Operating Officer of Cunard, Commodore R.W.Warwick, Captain of the *Queen Mary 2*, Stuart Perl, Director of Communications of Cunard GB, and his assistant, Matt Barrett. Thanks to our helicopter pilots: Eric Oger and Thierry Leygnac of Héli-Bretagne and Olivier Leborgne of Héli Blue (Martinique). Thanks to the City of Saint-Nazaire and its mayor, Joël Batteux, to Pilotage de Loire, for welcoming *Pêcheur d'images IV* into their installations, at the port authority and at the marina, not to mention the air traffic controllers at the Saint-Nazaire airport. Thanks to Éditions de La Martinière: to its president Hervé de La Martinière who gave us the means with which to create this publication, to Sabine Kuentz, our editor, to Olivier Fontvieille, for the art direction, and to Céline Moulard at Harry N. Abrams, Inc., New York. Thanks to Alain Lestienne of Le Govic who printed this project.

(LEFT TO RIGHT): Patrick Boissier, President and Chief Executive Officer of Alstom Chantiers de l'Atlantique, Pamela Conover, President and Chief Operating Officer of Cunard, Micky Arison, Chairman of the Board and Chief Executive Officer of the Carnival Corporation, the three artisans of this fabulous industrial adventure.

Photograph Credits
All the photographs in this book are by Philip Plisson, with the exception of:
Pages 66, 67, 68–69, 135–36, 143, 144–45, 152–53, 156, 157 (x3), 167, 194 (top), 196–97, 204–5, 222–23, 226–27, 229, 286–87, 288–89, 293 (x2), 296–97: Guillaume Plisson

Pages 4, 95 (x2), 112, 113, 114–15, 118, 123, 214, 216, 268, 275: Christophe Le Potier

Page 313 (center): with the generous permission of Cunard, London

Illustrations and photography archives:
Page 6: © Albert Brenet / ADAGP, Paris 2004
Pages 305–13 (except p. 313 [center]): with the generous permission of the Library of the University of Liverpool

You can find new images of the *Queen Mary 2* at www.plisson.com or write to philip@plisson.com.
All the photographs were taken with Canon EOS1 DS equipment and series L lenses.

Project Manager, English-language edition: Susan Richmond
Editor, English-language edition: Virginia Beck
Jacket design, English-language edition: Michael J Walsh Jr. and Christine Knorr
Design Coordinator, English-language edition: Makiko Ushiba
Production Coordinator, English-language edition: Kaija Markoe

Library of Congress Cataloging-in-Publication Data
Plisson, Philip.
Queen Mary 2 : the birth of a legend / Philip Plisson ; text by Gwen-Haël Denigot and Eric Flounders ; captions by Jean-Rémy Villageois and Philippe Kasse ; translated from the French by Simon Jones.
p. cm.
Includes bibliographical references and index.
ISBN 0-8109-5613-6 (hardcover)
1. Queen Mary 2 (Ship) I. Denigot, Gwen-Haël. II. Flounders, Eric. III. Title.

VM383.Q42P55 2004
387.5'42–dc22
2004007698

Published in 2004 by Harry N. Abrams, Incorporated, New York

Printed and bound in France
10 9 8 7 6 5 4 3 2 1

Harry N. Abrams, Inc.
100 Fifth Avenue
New York, N.Y. 10011
www.abramsbooks.com

Abrams is a subsidiary of